T0306124

The Volunteering Journey to Project Leadership

The project management profession has grown through the hard work of many volunteer groups and organizations. *The Volunteering Journey to Project Leadership* explains how volunteering can help project management professionals grow their own capabilities and careers. It explains how volunteering in project-oriented organizations, or any organization where projects are delivered, can help project managers develop leadership skills, build strong and diverse networks, and gain experiences in new fields. Any project manager or PMO can get advice and insights from this book, which explains how to:

- Identify volunteering goals that align with career goals
- Find the right organization that complements professional aspiration
- Choose activities for enhancing careers in project leadership
- Strategically select the right role to advance careers

Based on the authors' own volunteering and professional experiences, as well as interviews and informal discussion with more than 100 volunteers, this book is a hands-on guide to personal and professional growth in the field of project management. It is structured in three parts. Part I describes four ways volunteering can develop project leadership abilities. Part II focuses on leadership and adaptive skills, networking, and new skills gained by experimenting. Part III consolidates the learning and explains how to apply it at work. Each chapter ends with practical case studies, detailed interviews, key takeaways, and questions to reflect on.

Mayte Mata Sivera was born and raised in Xàbia, Spain. She is an experienced Project Management Office (PMO) Director based in Salt Lake City in the USA. With a master's degree in chemical engineering, Mayte has served as a project manager in the technology sector, overseeing projects around the world. Motivated by a passion for strategic and business development, Mayte pivoted her career trajectory to specialize as a project leader in these domains. This transition allowed her to contribute significantly to the strategic growth of organizations and align projects with their business objectives. She is committed to the project management community and is a dedicated board member at the Project Management Institute (PMI) Northern Utah chapter.

Yasmina Khelifi is a French telecom engineer and project manager with three PMI certifications. She has been working in the telecom industry for 20 years. She is a passionate volunteer at PMI. She is also a regular volunteer blogger on projectmanagement.com and a volunteer international correspondent at *PM World Journal*. She also writes in *Harvard Business Review Ascend*. She can speak six languages and has an MSc in Mobile Telecommunications. You can learn more about her work on her website: yasminakhelifi.com

The Volunteering Journey to Project Leadership
A Pathway to Improving Leadership Skills, Broadening Networks, and Exploring New Fields

Mayte Mata Sivera and Yasmina Khelifi

CRC Press
Taylor & Francis Group
Boca Raton London New York

CRC Press is an imprint of the
Taylor & Francis Group, an **informa** business

First edition published 2024
by CRC Press
2385 NW Executive Center Drive, Suite 320, Boca Raton FL 33431

and by CRC Press
4 Park Square, Milton Park, Abingdon, Oxon, OX14 4RN

CRC Press is an imprint of Taylor & Francis Group, LLC

ISBN: 9781032521503 (hbk)
ISBN: 9781032521497 (pbk)
ISBN: 9781003407942 (ebk)

DOI: 10.1201/9781003407942

Typeset in Times
by codeMantra

Contents

PART I   *Enhance Your Project Leadership by Volunteering*

PART II   *Develop Skills, Network, and Explore New Fields*

PART III   *Plan Your Career Development by Volunteering*

Acknowledgments

We are very grateful to all the volunteers we talked to who helped us learn and grow as project leaders. Mayte is thankful to the PMI Northern Utah chapter and TEDxSaltLakeCity. Yasmina is thankful to Dorie Clark and her wonderful REx community, the PMI France chapter, the PMI Germany chapter, the PMI UAE chapter, and PMI global volunteers.

Thank you to our excellent beta readers: Vicky Adams, Aalaa Aljar, Nart Abdullah, Cristina Baciu, Joelle Bejjani, Grateful N. Enyong-Eta, Franck Fadé, Chris Fenning, Erida Gervais, Rosa Gilsanz, Thabo Keamogetswe Masoka, Ilinca Nicolescu, Laure-Emmanuelle Peyret, Aaron Porter, Teresa Ramos Martin, Sonja Rueffer, and Renaud Taburiaux.

Thank you to the generous volunteers who agreed to share their stories: Fatimah Abbouchi, Badr Burshaid, Mazin Gadir, Luis Antonio Guardado Rivera, Rami Kaibni, Lee R. Lambert, Jonathan Lee, Jesus Martinez-Almela, Ayanda Nyikana, Paul Okeoghene Omugbe, Priya Patra, Ruth Pearce, Americo Pinto, Brigitte Schaden, and Raji Sivaraman.

Thank you to the thought leaders who agreed to provide an inspiring quotation: Joel Carboni, Dr Darius Danesh, Pierre Le Manh, Heidi Musser, Antonio Nieto-Rodriguez, Ike Nwankwo, David L. Pells, Joe Pusz, Amin Saidoun, and Ricardo Viana Vargas.

For their testimonies, we thank Nart Abdullah, Annesha Ahmed, Freddy Andale, Danny Byabene, Mark Cawood, Reece Dempster, Darkhantsetseg Erdenetsogt, Jennifer Fondrevay, Rosa Gilsanz, Maisa Husain, Rashad Issa, Brian Kemper, Becky Last, Billy S. Mwape, Ricardo Naciff, Nhung Nguyen, Yahaira Perez Jose, Barend Daniel Peters, Laure-Emmanuelle Peyret, Arief Prasetyo, Mac Prichard, Wan Syamilah Wan Ismail (Sya), and Ahmed Zouhair.

For their inspiring articles and books, we thank Christian Busch, Dorie Clark, and Irina Cozma.

Thank you to Elizabeth Borcia, Gorick Ng, Virginie Pires, Joe Pusz, and Manuel Souto-Otero for agreeing to be interviewed.

For their professional help, we thank Elizabeth Borcia, Abhirup Kondekar, Ravindra Kondekar, Florine de Korwin, and Kathleen McCully.

We are grateful to all volunteers and HR professionals who answered our surveys. Thank you to the people who helped us with the project: Jurgen Grotz, Laura Laseite, Maarten, Nelson Makokha Garissa, Vas S., and Gabriella Williams. Finally, we thank our friends and families for their support.

Self-Assessment

You may have picked up this book because you are a volunteer, or because you are interested in volunteering and would like to find out more about the subject. Before diving in, however, we suggest you take this self-assessment to find out more about your current attitudes to volunteering. For each question, you can select more than one option; you can grab a pen and paper to jot down some ideas to help you answer.

At the end of the book, we recommend you redo this self-assessment, updating it with the new ideas you've developed during your reading.

What is volunteering for you?

1. Giving back
2. A hobby
3. A professional development opportunity
4. A passion

Who is volunteering for?

1. Retired people
2. Young professionals
3. Any professional
4. Anyone

In what situations is volunteering suitable?

1. When you are unemployed
2. When you are self-employed
3. When you work in corporations
4. When you are transitioning from military to civilian life

Why are you volunteering or thinking about volunteering?

1. To gain leadership skills
2. To escape boredom at work
3. To work in other areas
4. To try out new things

What leadership skills can you enhance by volunteering?

1. Communication
2. Collaboration
3. Problem-solving
4. Strategic thinking

1 Introduction

By volunteering, you will learn lessons, meet colleagues, and reach accomplishments that you will hardly do in your professional career.

Antonio Nieto-Rodriguez
World Champion in Project Management

WHAT IS THIS BOOK ABOUT?

There are many worthwhile forms of volunteering that this book does not cover – like collecting donations for a charity or participating in a community cleanup. The book you hold is about acquiring and developing leadership skills, building a more robust network for today and tomorrow, and exploring new fields by contributing to, coordinating, or delivering projects as a volunteer, especially in project management organizations. You can still apply what you learn to other organizations that deliver projects, but the experiences described and the examples given in this book primarily concern volunteering in project management organizations.

When we talk about project management organizations, we are referring to organizations like the Project Management Institute (PMI), the International Project Management Association (IPMA), the PMO Global Alliance (PMOGA),[1] the PMO Leader, the Australian Institute of Project Management (AIPM), the Association of Change Management Professionals (ACMP), the International Institute of Business Analysis (IIBA), or any related organization or chapter in your country.

In this book, we will use the term **projectized organizations** to encompass them all.

WHY THIS BOOK?

We, the authors of this book, have been project leaders for decades and have volunteered for years in different projectized organizations. To our surprise, we have been able to capitalize on our volunteering experiences to strengthen our leadership skills at work: for example, we gained the confidence to advocate for our work projects in front of diverse audiences, something we would never have thought we could do. As you read our book, you will become aware of all the transferable skills you can gain through volunteering. You'll navigate the world of volunteering with a fresh perspective and enjoy it more.

WHO IS THIS BOOK FOR?

You are an aspirant project manager, or a junior or even a seasoned project manager. You are a program manager, a portfolio manager, or a PMO director. In other words, you are a **project leader**.

You might have earned diplomas in project management, obtained a project management certification, or accrued several years of project experience. Regardless of

DOI: 10.1201/9781003407942-1

your situation or industry, you must acquire, practice, and maintain leadership skills. You know you need to build connections. You understand you need to learn new things to deliver your projects. But today, learning is not just a formal activity carried out in classrooms.[2] Learning means practicing, collaborating with people, and experimenting with new things. And sometimes this is not possible in your day job. You might have found yourself wondering:

- How can you learn or strengthen skills you don't practice at work?
- How can you collaborate with diverse people?
- How can you discover new things?

The answer is volunteering, and this book will guide you.

This book is for project leaders of all career stages who want to improve their leadership skills, expand their network, and explore new fields by volunteering. Doing these things will elevate your employability as a project leader and prepare you for the future. Throughout the book, you will be provided with frameworks and guidance if you are a new or aspiring volunteer. If you are already a seasoned volunteer, you will be encouraged to reflect on your current paths and future volunteering engagements. You will also get inspiration and insights into mentoring new volunteers.

This book results from our personal experiences and from numerous discussions with worldwide volunteers. Over the years, we surveyed over 100 volunteers to understand how they gained leadership skills, amplified their networks, and explored new fields by volunteering.

If you're ready to shape your future in project leadership, let's dive in.

HOW IS THIS BOOK STRUCTURED?

Although the chapters are self-contained, we recommend reading them in order, because they follow a skill-building trajectory: you select a skill to learn, look for an appropriate volunteer role, and bring the skill back into your workplace to support your journey to project leadership.

The book is structured in three parts:

- Part I: Enhance your project leadership by volunteering.
- Part II: Develop skills, network, and explore new fields.
- Part III: Plan your career development by volunteering.

PART I: Enhance your project leadership by volunteering.

Chapter 2 will introduce the topic and explain how volunteering can help you become a better project leader in four ways. You'll also find a useful tool we designed, My Volunteering Canvas, to help you align your goals with your volunteer roles.

PART II: Develop skills, network, and explore new fields.

Chapter 3 will cover six leadership skills you can learn and sharpen by volunteering:

- leadership styles
- communication

FIGURE 1.1 Four Steps of Skill Development by Volunteering

- collaboration
- motivation
- problem-solving
- strategic thinking

Chapter 4 will help you enhance your adaptive skills. You will learn to:

- manage your time
- manage organizational expectations
- manage your commitment level
- prevent burnout
- handle conflicts
- tame your ego

In both chapters, we will examine what each skill brings and how to learn, practice, and transfer it to your work environment (Figure 1.1).

Chapter 5 will advise you on networking for your current and future job.

Chapter 6 will show you the power of experimenting, gaining credibility in new fields, and leveraging it for your personal brand.

Chapter 7 will help you remain employable in four situations: unemployment, self-employment, working in corporations, and transitioning from military life.

PART III Plan your career development by volunteering.

In Chapters 8–13, you will learn to identify your goals so that you can choose the most appropriate organization, activity, and volunteer role. By the end of the book, you'll know how to transfer what you have learned back into your project leadership role.

At the end of each chapter, you'll find:

- a case study
- a volunteer's story
- key takeaways

These will help you think about your volunteering journey and the learning you get out of it.

Throughout the book, you'll hear how volunteering has made a difference in the careers and lives of project leaders worldwide. While you read the examples and personal histories, we encourage you to keep a journal to help you reflect on how you can apply this knowledge in your own volunteer and project leadership roles. All stories and case studies are based on real examples, but in some cases the details and identities of volunteers have been changed to protect their privacy. When this is the case, we will use * after the name. The names of firms in the case studies are not the real ones, and any likeness to the name of a genuine firm is coincidental.

Each volunteer's story contains more detailed testimony of how volunteering impacted one project leader's professional and personal life.

Finally, the key takeaways will challenge you to think about your current and future volunteering engagements by taking an A.H.A. (activity, hope, action) moment:

- Activity: Three questions will help you think about what you learned from the current chapter.
- Hope: Take time to express what you want to achieve based on the information provided in the chapter. A prompt will be provided to guide you.
- Action: Turn your hope into one concrete action to advance your career.

By the end of this book, we hope to equip you with all you need to have fun volunteering and, at the same time, grow as a project leader.

NOTES

1 During the writing of this book, it was announced that PMI had acquired PMOGA; all testimonies, surveys, and comments were gathered before the acquisition.
2 Hoffman, R., Yeh, C., & Casnocha, B. (2019). Learn from People, Not Classes: Whom Do You Know, and What Can They Teach You? *Harvard Business Review*, 94(3), 54–61. https://hbr.org/2019/03/learn-from-people-not-classes

Part I

*Enhance Your Project
Leadership by Volunteering*

2 Four Ways Volunteering Can Help to Develop Your Project Leadership Career

Volunteers are at the core of PMI's global community, fueling our passion, engagement, unity, and commitment to improve project management. Volunteering is about giving back to others. But volunteering at PMI is also a unique school of leadership, providing project professionals with a multitude of opportunities to develop their skills, broaden their network, and deliver positive impact to the world.

Pierre Le Manh
PMI President and CEO

Before we dig deeper into the four ways project volunteering can help you develop your project leadership career, let's first understand what project volunteering means.

PROJECT VOLUNTEERING IS CONTRIBUTING YOUR TIME AND SKILLS TO COMPLETE A PROJECT

Project volunteering involves contributing your time and skills for free to support, deliver, or lead a project outside of work. It's an opportunity to collaborate with peers to impact the community significantly. Project volunteering can take many forms: building a community garden, organizing an educational program for underprivileged young people, participating in projectized organizations, mentoring, supporting a nonprofit with their social media, or organizing a training course, a webinar, or an annual event. You can find project volunteering roles in projectized organizations. Many of them are not-for-profit organizations that are eager to get volunteers. You can be a member of more than one projectized organization and thereby contribute to different kinds of projects and initiatives. Nart, a French-Jordanian project manager, told us:

> Volunteering at the PMI France chapter was an eye-opening experience. That was the first time I understood what project volunteering meant. Before, I volunteered to give blood or in a local folklore festival to keep my culture alive. I began by giving webinars to share my knowledge about Agile. When people asked me questions, I realized my contribution was valuable. I also learned through their questions and different perspectives. It boosted my morale when I felt stuck at work and helped me acquire skills beyond the work sphere (e.g., using new software). I could also work with some retired project leaders and learn from their experiences in projects and life.

DOI: 10.1201/9781003407942-3

Like Nart, project volunteering will help you to develop your project leadership career in four ways:

- leadership skills development
- networking
- exploration of new fields
- employability

DEVELOP YOUR LEADERSHIP SKILLS

You have a unique advantage as a project leader, because you can use your project management skills to address specific issues and create lasting solutions that benefit the community for years. When you volunteer to deliver a project, you lead and collaborate with people to reach a common goal in an environment where you need to quickly grasp the organizational constraints, sometimes without formal onboarding or clear explanations. And you don't have the whole day to figure things out, because you're doing this in addition to your paid job. You need to analyze the challenges in the projects and find proper solutions, sometimes on the fly. You learn by doing in an informal context. You are not in a university classroom. You manage projects with friends, and with lower stakes than at work. It can give you more freedom and confidence to practice and try out leadership skills.

Here are two situations that you may face as a project leader:

- You want to learn and practice leadership skills you are not using yet.
- You want to improve your existing leadership skills but don't get to practice them enough in your current job.

As we will see in Part II, volunteering will help you in both situations. You must choose the appropriate organization, roles, and activities to maximize the benefits of volunteering. We will talk about that in Part III.

One thing is sure: you'll get to meet many new people.

DEVELOP YOUR NETWORK

Projectized organizations bring together diverse audiences. Volunteers come from different academic and social backgrounds, with various life histories, and from other corporate cultures, industries, or countries. Some projectized organizations operate nationwide, or even worldwide.

By delivering projects, you'll get to know your peers better. You'll get to interact with them in an informal setting. These collaborations will help you build a network of friends and colleagues you wouldn't have met otherwise. You'll gain new job market insights and learn about companies or industries you hadn't previously considered. Additionally, expanding your network will help you to discover and learn about new fields.

Ricardo Naciff, project senior consultant, PMI France chapter past president, told us: "I was born in Argentina, where volunteering can sound very strange. Work for free? Why? This is not too smart, isn't it? But the payback is not about money but experience and networking."

EXPLORE NEW FIELDS

Volunteering will open up new avenues for you. You can discover other companies, industries, and hiring managers that are looking for their new project leaders. For example, if you volunteer in the partnership or outreach team of an organization, you will be at the core of the discussions with potential partners. Besides, in the volunteering setting, you may be more open to exploring new things or participating in activities than you are in the workplace. For example, you may find the confidence to create visuals for social media, whereas, at work, you might not dare to attempt this kind of activity because you have to prioritize project deadlines and performance objectives. You can volunteer to speak at a panel discussion, whereas, at work, you might not be allowed to share your knowledge publicly. You can also discover new areas of interest and new strengths. It can lead you to steer your career in new directions you would never have imagined. By doing so, you will remain employable.

STAY EMPLOYABLE

Skills development, networking, and exploring new fields contribute to your employability. No one can rely on having a career for life anymore. Macroeconomics and the speed of technological and societal changes influenced that shift. Today, you need to learn to navigate between roles, responsibilities, and enterprises by acquiring and practicing transferable skills, nurturing your networks, and having the courage to experiment. By volunteering, you'll find yourself going beyond your qualifications, day job, and work experiences as a project leader. As one of the volunteers we surveyed summarized it: "Volunteering has helped with career development in different ways such as skill development, networking opportunities, demonstrating commitment, filling employment gaps, exploring career options, and building a positive reputation." Another told us: "It has given me vital contacts, skills, knowledge and has made me more well-rounded." You will also improve your ability to adapt to an unpredictable world.

Let's turn now to a concrete visual tool to help you navigate your volunteering journey, irrespective of whether you are a new or experienced volunteer.

MY VOLUNTEERING CANVAS

We want to give you a practical tool: My Volunteering Canvas (Figure 2.1).[1]

You can download My Volunteering Canvas on our website (https://volunteer2leader.my.canva.site/).

Before applying for an opportunity, prefill the sections you can with your preferences and expectations. During your communications with the organization, update the information.

Use this canvas as your compass during your tenure to check that your goals, activities, and roles are still aligned.

At the end of your tenure, summarize what you learned and improved.

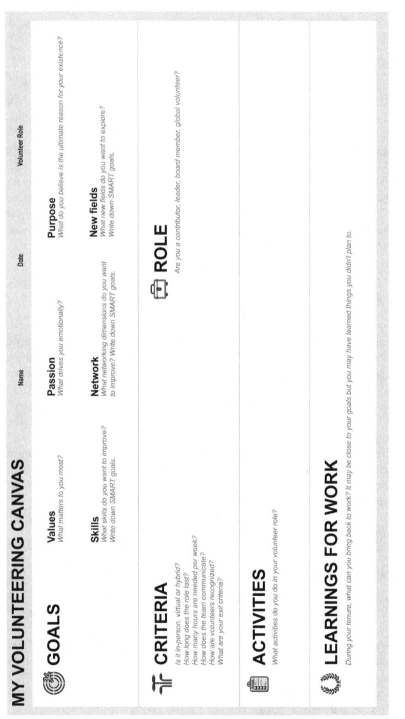

MY VOLUNTEERING CANVAS

Name   Date   Volunteer Role

🎯 GOALS

Values
What matters to you most?

Skills
What skills do you want to improve?
Write down SMART goals.

Passion
What drives you emotionally?

Network
What networking dimensions do you want
to improve? Write down SMART goals.

Purpose
What do you believe is the ultimate reason for your existence?

New fields
What new fields do you want to explore?
Write down SMART goals.

💼 ROLE

Are you a contributor, leader, board member, global volunteer?

CRITERIA

Is it in-person, virtual or hybrid?
How long does the role last?
How many hours are needed per week?
How does the team communicate?
How are volunteers recognized?
What are your exit criteria?

⬛ ACTIVITIES

What activities do you do in your volunteer role?

🌿 LEARNINGS FOR WORK

During your tenure, what can you bring back to work? It may be close to your goals but you may have learned things you didn't plan to.

FIGURE 2.1   My Volunteering Canvas

While reading the book, you can complete or modify the canvas at any point in your journey. You may find it especially useful when reading Part III.

In the coming chapters, you can fill in the canvas when you see this symbol: ▣

CASE STUDY: VOLUNTEERING IS NOT VALUED IN MY COUNTRY. IS IT STILL WORTHWHILE?

Monique* is a French project leader with five years of experience, working in an American firm in France. Her American colleagues have regularly mentioned to her that it would be good to volunteer in a project management organization to network, learn, and give back to the community. Monique is skeptical because volunteering is not valued in the workplace in France, and none of her French colleagues are volunteering. What is volunteering going to bring her? It is also unpaid. How can she devote time to unpaid activities when she already faces challenges in maintaining a work–life balance?

When she talked to her manager about the possibility of volunteering, he said, "That's fine, as long as it doesn't affect your primary job." But he did not encourage her, nor was he particularly enthusiastic.

Should Monique volunteer, even though it is not valued in her country or workplace?

Our Views

Yes, Monique should give it a try. She could begin with a very well-defined and short or one-off activity to evaluate whether she likes it. Also, she should remember her manager's view that the activity shouldn't impact her day-to-day job.

We relate to Monique's indecision. We are both from cultures and academic backgrounds where volunteering does not bring value to our curriculum vitae (CV) or resume. And yet, through volunteering, we have learned a lot, and we do not regret it. Taking the leap requires courage and an understanding of your motivations. People's motivations to get involved are diverse. For some, their employer must value volunteering. For others, the joy of learning or making new friends is the core motivation. Monique, who is still skeptical, might discover a real passion for volunteering by trying it out.

VOLUNTEERS' STORIES: JESUS MARTINEZ-ALMELA IN SPAIN

Jesus Martinez-Almela is a professional engineer and certified projects portfolio director. He has volunteered for over 30 years with AEIPRO-IPMA SPAIN (Asociación Española de Dirección e Ingeniería de Proyectos-International Project Management Association). From a young age, he was involved in youth associations, and when he started to work, it was natural for him to volunteer in engineering or project organizations. He carried out different activities.

From 1993 to date, in Spain, as a volunteer, he led a professional worldwide accredited Certification Body in Spain. "I have had the honor of contributing in different fields, membership, education and training, research, and standards. I have been World Vice President, World President, and Chairman of the Council at IPMA (from 2005 to 2023)." When his journey with IPMA stops, he will return to being an individual volunteer without great worldwide responsibilities. Titles are not necessary. What is important is to contribute to a good cause, to help others, and to generate better things.

Jesus admits that helping others is also an exercise in healthy selfishness because it makes the volunteer feel good. But beyond this, volunteering has helped Jesus know himself and how to handle himself.

"Leading others begins with knowing how to manage yourself and leading by example. I help others to make it possible by collaborating." For Jesus, this is one of the main benefits of volunteering. "You know yourself through learning and improving your attitude with others."

He has given his time, know-how, and competence without expecting anything in return. What drives him is the value he can generate for others; this is where volunteering differs from paid work.

> I was lucky enough to be able to receive that compensation of gratitude from the people and organizations to which I contributed as a volunteer; there have been many good, satisfactory cases, helping to create hope and expectations, helping to train people, leading by example, in more than 40 countries … for more than 30 years.

He has had the opportunity to meet many people, which has kept him curious and open to differences. He has built bridges with worldwide peers – some of whom are now close friends – to generate competences. "Everything evolves … in our complex world. The important thing is not to know but to know how to connect with people, how to solve problems together, and above all, for me, to know how to behave."

When we asked him when he would stop, he was surprised. He wants to keep on helping future generations to embark on this volunteering path to change the world together. "In the 21st century, societies need more good people, more committed people, helping to create a fairer, more free and more inclusive world, more projects for … society instead of only for business and the economy itself."

KEY TAKEAWAYS

- Project volunteering means contributing your time and skills to complete a project.
- You'll learn to tailor your leadership skills.
- You'll expand your network.
- You'll get hands-on experience in new areas.

YOUR A.H.A. MOMENT: ACTIVITY, HOPE, ACTION

It's your turn!

ACTIVITY

Answer the questions below:

- What leadership skills would you like to develop?
- Why do you want to build your network?
- What new field would you like to explore?

HOPE

What do you hope to grow in your career by volunteering?
Prompt: "By volunteering, I hope to grow my career in this way: ..."

ACTION

Write down an action you want to take to start or improve your volunteer journey.

NOTE

1 We designed My Volunteering Canvas inspired by the Business Model Canvas by Alexander Osterwalder and the Project Canvas by Antonio Nieto-Rodriguez.

Part II

Develop Skills, Network, and Explore New Fields

3 Develop Your Leadership Skills

Volunteering is a gift that has taught me about empathy and compassion, and it's allowed me to learn how to ask for help – THE core leadership discipline.

Heidi Musser
Board Member, Board Advisor, Executive Consultant, TEDx Speaker

In PMI's Pulse of the Profession® 2023 report, project professionals "rated communication, problem-solving, collaborative leadership, and strategic thinking as the most critical power skills [i.e. soft skills] in helping them fulfill organizational objectives."[1]

In this chapter, you'll learn, practice, and transfer six crucial leadership skills (some mentioned above and others identified from our own experience):

- Tailor your leadership style.
- Master your communication.
- Collaborate better.
- Motivate teams.
- Improve your problem-solving.
- Strengthen your strategic thinking.

TAILOR YOUR LEADERSHIP STYLE

Understand the Benefits

Leadership styles are how you lead, inspire people, and get things done, regardless of the environment and the person you need to collaborate with. As a project leader, you have your own preferred leadership styles, ways of tackling problems, collaborating, and motivating people. These might be the ones your team members prefer too – or not.

What if you don't adapt your leadership style? What will you miss out on?

Most project leaders don't have direct authority over their team members and stakeholders. If you don't understand how to engage with them, you will demotivate them, and progress will stall. Volunteering in a projectized organization can help you because it is an accelerated leadership laboratory. It will allow you to observe different leadership styles and see which styles work best with whom. You can hone your preferred leadership styles, and, at the same time, you can try out other leadership styles you are uncomfortable with at work in a safe environment. Adjusting your style is even more critical here because volunteers are freer to give up their role without explanation. Their commitment and motivation to help will depend on the relationships you've built with them. When you tailor your leadership style to the

DOI: 10.1201/9781003407942-5

requirements of your team members and the situation, you build trust, because you are listening to what your team members need. And trust will fuel their motivation to move the project forward. If one team member needs more autonomy to innovate and you micro manage them, it will stifle their creativity. It will create conflict, and they may leave eventually.

Finding the best leadership style to fit the situation will pave the way to solving problems and adapting to changing circumstances. Let's find out about some common leadership styles that you can practice.

FOUR LEADERSHIP STYLES

Let us briefly review four common leadership styles and their main characteristics:

- Authoritative or directive: is a firm leadership style with clear instructions and minimal collaboration
- Coaching: supports growth, provides encouragement, and develops through personalized mentorship and guidance
- Delegative or laissez-faire leadership: gives initiatives to team members
- Participative or democratic: involves people in the decision-making process, puts people's needs first, and helps them develop themselves

Have you identified your preferred leadership styles? Which ones do you use most often?

By volunteering, you can experiment and try the ones you usually don't use, as well as improving the ones you are more familiar with.

VOLUNTEERING IS YOUR PRACTICE LABORATORY

You don't need to be a prominent team leader or a board member to practice leadership in a volunteering role. But you need to create the right conditions for your practice to thrive:

- Stop doing tasks for your teams. They may need ongoing advice and reassurance, but they need to figure out how to solve problems themselves.
- Accept that doing things differently from how you usually do them can still be successful.
- Acknowledge that success relies on being adaptable.

If your volunteer role involves, for example, managing a membership database, you may have fewer opportunities to tailor your leadership styles, but will certainly acquire valuable technical skills. We advise collaborating with at least two other volunteers to practice your leadership skills.

Accept opportunities to work with new people. Sometimes, the temptation in volunteering is to create projects with friends and to lock yourself in your bubble. However, if you want to challenge yourself and hone your leadership styles, we highly recommend you engage in a volunteer opportunity that will allow you to work with new people, people who are at different stages in their professional careers or who belong to various industries. For example, imagine you lead a marketing campaign in a nonprofit organization. In your role, you lead a team utilizing diverse leadership styles. Recognizing one volunteer's autonomy, you adopt a laissez-faire approach, guiding as needed to nurture their creativity and independence. For another volunteer who values collaboration, you employ a democratic leadership style, fostering open communication and collective decision-making to cultivate a sense of ownership and teamwork. These volunteering experiences will nurture your leadership styles in the workplace.

TRANSFER TO YOUR PROJECT LEADER ROLE

Look online for a leadership assessment that you can take to understand or confirm your preferred leadership styles.[2]

When you have had the opportunity to experiment with different leadership styles through volunteering, you must evaluate the best leadership styles to bring back into your workplace. It will depend on what stage your team is at. According to a commonly used framework created by Bruce W. Tuckman, the development of teams has four stages[3]:

- forming
- storming
- norming
- performing

At the forming stage, the team gets to know each other. The leader must be more directive to structure the team and give clarity. At the storming stage, the team collaborates and voices their opinions. Conflicts may arise. A coaching leadership style is required. At the norming stage, the group makes progress. The leader can loosen the reins. A supporting collaborative form of leadership, like the participative style, is more appropriate. At the performing stage, the team is a high-performing one. The leader can delegate more and start preparing their succession plan.

Then, you also need to tailor your leadership style to your team's individual needs. This will depend on their learning curve. When you work with experts, the authoritative leadership style will not work. A participative style will be better. However, if you are working with new team members, some of them will like a more directive leadership style.

For example, in a volunteering role, Yasmina used an authoritative leadership style to get information and move the project forward. It didn't work well, because the volunteers were experienced and therefore more resistant to this leadership style. A few months later, Yasmina took a new job replacing a contractor, and she decided to create more structured project documentation. She tried to get as much information as possible, observe, and take time to understand the context. She used the lessons learned from volunteering: joining a new team or beginning a new job means watching, not evaluating too quickly, and being patient.

So, she has shifted her mindset from acting to listening.

Thanks to her numerous volunteer roles, Mayte also had to change her perspective. At a local TEDx event, she was well known for rolling up her sleeves, unloading trucks, filling water bottles, and running errands – but she didn't have the time to do it all. By focusing on the minor details, she lost sight of the big picture, creating frustration within the team. She had to change her focus from doing to leading.

Also, she has learned the importance of delegating well to be a good leader. Through volunteering, she practiced assigning tasks to other team members, empowering the team, and keeping them accountable. This new leadership skill helped her to make a career transition, to operations, after more than ten years in technology.

Project leadership is getting things done by people not under your authority. It's not about doing everything by yourself. It's not about giving orders. It's about influencing people to collaborate efficiently. And mastering your communication is essential.

MASTER YOUR COMMUNICATION

COMMUNICATION SKILLS

Communication can be oral, written, nonverbal (body language), or paraverbal (tone, voice). Communication skills are essential for effective and inspiring leadership.

Ask yourself: are your communication skills strong enough? If not, you can find yourself facing misunderstandings, leading to delays or setbacks, or conflicts because you are not using the same language or vocabulary as your team. You need to have the ability to adjust your communication style so that you can collaborate effectively with all team members, not just those who happen to share a communication style that is similar to yours.

When you master the art of communication, you tailor your message (words and language) and the format (voice and tone) to the person you talk to. Effectively communicating with a supply chain director is distinct from leading a meeting with the finance controller. Effective communication involves understanding the unique communication needs of different team members.

COMMUNICATION CAN BE LEARNED

Recognizing whether you need to improve your communication skills is the first step. Do you need help expressing your ideas or writing emails? Do you find it difficult to influence others and justify your views? If you have experienced communication problems in the past, for each situation, take a moment to analyze what went wrong, what feedback you got, and what you can improve.

However, if you are convinced you have strong communication skills, you can still find opportunities to develop them even further in volunteering settings.

Whether you are gaining new skills or developing existing ones, you can benefit from creating a learning plan specifically focused on improving your communication. Here are some elements you could include:

- Read and expand your knowledge.
- Take a communication assessment to identify the areas you need to improve.
- Enroll in a communication course.

- Participate in an intercultural course.
- Take a class on writing business English or another language you want to improve.
- Observe and learn from effective communicators that match your style.
- Leverage technology, record yourself, and identify areas for improvement.
- Join public speaking clubs (like Toastmasters).

Here are some other factors to consider in your learning plan:

- Observe how people communicate in projectized organizations: do they prefer emails? Informal messaging? Phone calls?
- Assess the gaps between your own communication preferences and the ones used in the organization.
- Analyze the communication requirements needed in your volunteer role. Will you be giving presentations? Are you going to write documents? Will you interact with your team, other teams, or international teams?

Maybe you are convinced you don't have a natural inclination toward effective communication. But anyone can develop excellent communication skills, and practice is the key.

Seize Opportunities to Practice

Before looking for the perfect volunteer opportunity to practice your communication skills, you need to embrace these three principles:

- Focus on a few specific skills. Communication is a vast domain, and you cannot improve everything simultaneously. For example, you could focus on tone and gestures.
- Seek feedback and mentorship. Ask for feedback on your communication skills from trusted colleagues, mentors, or supervisors.
- Self-reflect on your progress.

Volunteering will allow you to practice communication in every interaction. You must deliver projects with people you have never met and perhaps will never meet face-to-face. Or perhaps you will collaborate with them after having only talked briefly with them. You must deploy more influence and conviction to accomplish things when people are not being paid for their efforts.

Here are some standard guidelines on how to convey an impactful message, which you can practice in a volunteer setting and then apply to your day-to-day activities or work:

- Frame the context of the interaction in the first minute.[4] People have different information than you. Taking a few seconds to explain things at the start will avoid wasting time later. It is even more crucial in volunteering, where people may not have straightforward onboarding or know the organization's jargon.

- Be clear and concise. It will help you remove ambiguity and avoid problems. Select your language thoughtfully, and keep it straightforward. If the language is not your native language, use software to correct your writing or ask for clarifications when you speak. For example, you can volunteer to write social media posts and request a mentor to review them.
- Consider the intercultural aspects of communication. Different cultures may have different attitudes to pauses between words, interruptions, and direct or indirect ways of expressing requests or raising issues.

You may have to make a public presentation in your volunteer role. If so:

- Start with a compelling opening. You should practice starting your presentations or meetings with a strong statement to set the tone and establish credibility.
- Tell stories. Stories will help to illustrate complex ideas and create emotions. People will relate to them.
- Use positive body language. Nonverbal communication accounts for a significant part of the message. Pay attention to it. When you attend conferences, observe the body language of the speakers. You can look at webinars without sound so that you can concentrate on the presenters' body language.
- Practice and rehearse your next presentation, paying particular attention to timing and pacing. Speaking and presenting at an appropriate pace will ensure that your stakeholders or attendees of your presentation understand your message, and rehearsing in advance will increase your confidence.
- Use simple visuals. Clear and simple visuals enhance comprehension and information retention. During your volunteering journey, you are likely to see many presentations. Make a note of your favorite visuals and ask their creators how they made them.

During each interaction in your volunteer opportunities, there are some principles you should always follow, regardless of whether you are a team leader or an individual contributor:

- Practice active listening. It will help you build positive relationships and develop your empathy. Show that you can listen to another person without sharing your opinion or advice. When you don't understand someone's behavior, take the time to talk openly with that person and find out their underlying reasons.
- Encourage participation in your teams. If you plan to review a document at a meeting, send it to team members in advance, so they will have time to read it before the meeting. During a meeting, observe the silent team members and give them the opportunity to provide feedback in the chat or orally. Facilitate conversations.

Look for roles where effective communication is pivotal, such as mentoring, community outreach, or public presentations. For instance, mentoring involves articulating ideas clearly and empathetically. Community outreach necessitates engaging diverse audiences and refining verbal and written communication skills. Suppose public speaking is your weakness; whenever possible, volunteer to speak in public and present the project's status, or welcome participants to a face-to-face event. Or present in meetings. Opting for such roles allows you to practice and enhance communication skills that are applicable to your professional development.

That is precisely what Ran* did.

Ran was initially shy. Then, he began to volunteer and found himself in a role where he needed to talk in front of others. His first attempts were challenging. However, he prepared and rehearsed. The practice and the experiment in the volunteer role paid off, as the more he talked, the more he felt comfortable speaking to colleagues at work, from junior professionals to executives.

TRANSFER TO YOUR PROJECT LEADER ROLE

If you consciously apply your communication skills in your project leader role, you can create a positive, collaborative, and productive environment. Think of the lessons learned during your volunteering engagements. What can you transfer to work? To help you, here are some situations where you can transfer the communication skills you have learned:

- effective delegation
- conflict resolution (which we will discuss later)
- stakeholder management
- persuasion
- motivation and engagement

You can listen actively, lead by example, and exchange with your team members in your work situations.

Active listening in a professional setting sometimes involves overriding your first instincts: for example, when a developer explains a bug, it's easy to brainstorm solutions based on your experiences immediately. But hold back. Instead, listen, reformulate, and keep an open mind, instead of jumping ahead to the solutions.

Lead by example: is there an online communication course you've taken part in that you can recommend to the team? Chat in one-on-one meetings not only about technical expertise but also about communication. By trying to master your communication, you are on the right track to create better collaborative relationships.

COLLABORATE BETTER

UNDERSTAND THE BENEFITS

Effective collaboration means being able to listen to other perspectives (even if you disagree), to understand the thought process (even if you don't want to), and to think of how this new perspective will benefit the project (even if your ego is damaged).

Let's imagine you are not convinced about the importance of collaboration. You may think you can do everything yourself because you are competent. And it will be quicker and more efficient. But soon, you will be overwhelmed and need your peers' help. You will need to explain the project's vision to these people in a hurry. They will have to ask you questions to find out how they can help. And these late explanations may translate into delays in project delivery.

The essence of a project is collaboration. As a project leader, it is crucial to improve your collaboration skills, especially if you realize that these are currently undeveloped. Effective collaboration relies a lot on the communication skills we have talked about earlier, but these alone are not enough.

LEARN TO COLLABORATE BETTER

If you are an individual contributor or used to working independently, you will need to look for volunteer opportunities that expose you to teamwork. These opportunities may have the following characteristics:

- sharing responsibilities
- collaborative decision-making
- balancing dependencies and priorities: if you work in a team, you will need to understand the big picture, which means understanding your and other people's preferences and balancing them properly. If you are used to working with a collocated team, try to contribute to a project with remote members.

On the other hand, if you are used to making decisions and being part of the strategy, you must expose yourself to opportunities where you are not the leader; you are within a larger group, supporting and assisting rather than making decisions.

Regardless of your experience so far, you can become a better collaborative leader with effort and practice.

SEEK CROSS-FUNCTIONAL PROJECTS

Practice is essential for becoming a more collaborative leader. However, to make the most of it, you need to acknowledge three key aspects:

- Project collaboration is not a battle to get people to agree with every word you say.
- Project collaboration does not delay things.
- Project collaboration is a way to develop diverse perspectives.

During your volunteering journey, you will collaborate with a myriad of people, whether new or seasoned volunteers. You are going to lead a multitude of projects, big or small. You'll have assigned projects, and you'll contribute to others. When searching for volunteer roles, it's a good idea to pick ones where you work with different teams. For example, being an event project manager means collaborating with people in the areas of technology, marketing, communications, and partnerships. There are also other projects, such as contributing to a newsletter or developing an organization's mobile application.

This kind of cross-collaboration will help you learn from different approaches and meet new people. Also, once you've chosen a volunteer role, it's important to ask for feedback on whether others see you as someone who works well with others. This way, you can make sure you're a good team player and getting the most value out of your volunteer role.

Reece Dempster told us that becoming a better collaborator takes time and effort. Reece is the Western Australia (WA) Chapter president at the AIPM. He has found there are two critical fundamental inputs into not-for-profit organizations: human resources and physical assets (budget and locations). "In my experience," he said, "a leader's ability to collaborate, engage and drive participation from the team is critical. This lesson was learned early and I have been exploring ways to manifest this in all my teams."[5]

First, with his team, he identifies a specific relatable reason why the team is doing what they are doing, which is normally a subset of the organization's mission statement ("The WA Chapter Council will engage and participate with members through advocacy, virtual environments, and face-to-face events so that AIPM's vision and values are realized").

Second, through his reading, he has discovered that a person is at balance when, on average, they are assigned goals and responsibilities that equal 100 hours a year.

Third, he set targets that are hard to achieve but easy to work towards; the targets are not treated as a must-achieve but a continuous work in progress.

Fourth, working with trust and intention towards the agreed goals is essential. He advocates having a "leader of leaders" mindset, in recognition of that small percentage of intrinsically motivated people who actively support the community for free. He has slowly been implementing these strategies over the last 12 months with success.

"Volunteering has allowed me to practice implementing these and other strategies that have greatly improved our collective ability to collaborate and achieve our goals as well as greatly helping my professional career in my paid position as a project manager," said Reece.

Transfer to Your Project Leader Role

At work, you should focus on three aspects:

- Foster a culture of collaboration in your teams, for example, by sharing knowledge.
- Facilitate effective teamwork: remove roadblocks and address conflicts at the right time.
- Define decision-making processes and who is part of them.

Have regular meetings with the project team on improving collaboration: do you need new tools? Do you need to define new processes? Do you need to talk about behaviors?

You can also look for opportunities in your department to create best practices on collaborations and contribute to knowledge forums. Participate in Employee Resource Groups (ERGs) or cross-functional projects. That will help you understand different perspectives and enrich your empathy capital, which will help you motivate your teams.

MOTIVATE TEAMS

UNDERSTAND THE BENEFITS

As a project leader, you must discover what motivates your team members and align their motivations with the project's goals.

Think for a minute. Do you understand how to motivate your team? In the volunteering setting, people are often moved by the desire to help others. This desire in itself will keep them motivated. Or in more technical volunteering fields, experts may remain motivated by the recognition they get from others. These intrinsic motivations can work for a while, but there may come a point where something additional is needed.

When you take time to understand what drives and motivates your team, and what gives their work a meaningful purpose, you will find it easier to engage them in contributing to and delivering projects. But first we need to look at the underlying theories.

MOTIVATIONAL THEORIES

Here are some proven theories of motivation that we would like to highlight:

- Herzberg's motivation-hygiene (or two-factor) theory
- the self-determination theory (SDT) of Deci and Ryan
- Daniel Pink's elements of intrinsic motivations
- Patrick Lencioni's factors

Frederick Herzberg, together with his collaborators Mausner and Snyderman, developed the motivation-hygiene theory.[6] According to this theory, hygiene factors create demotivation if they are not met. Hygiene factors include salary, work conditions, job security, and status. Motivators relate to achievement, responsibility, learning, and recognition.

The psychologists Edward Deci and Richard Ryan developed the SDT, which supports this view.[7] Extrinsic motivations stem from external rewards (monetary, social recognition) or punishments (shame). You have intrinsic motivations when you do things for your inherent satisfaction, pleasure, enjoyment, and personal development. You feel intrinsically motivated because you achieve and learn something through these activities. Intrinsic motivations also come from the autonomy and control you have over what you are doing.

Research has shown that extrinsic motivations give short-term satisfaction, while intrinsic motivations provide long-term satisfaction. More recent theories shed further light on this.

Daniel Pink's book *Drive* builds on the SDT.[8] He identifies three elements of intrinsic motivations:

- Autonomy: We want to direct our lives.
- Mastery: We want to be better at things that matter.
- Purpose: We want to do things that serve bigger goals.

Patrick Lencioni, in his book *Three Signs of a Miserable Job*, looks at three core factors contributing to unhappiness in the workplace[9]:

- Anonymity: People need to be known and not only by their work achievements.
- Irrelevance: People need to see how their activities make a difference in the lives of others.
- Immeasurement (a term Lencioni came up with himself): People need to assess their own performance and have clear evidence of their outcomes, independently of their managers' opinions or other influential people.

These theories have a common point: you need to understand the individual motives of your team members and that different things motivate (or demotivate) people.

MOTIVATING TEAMS INVOLVES A SHARED VISION AND PURPOSE

We must acknowledge that motivating teams in a volunteer setting is far more complex than at work. Volunteers can leave your project quickly if they are no longer interested or have time. Billy S. Mwape, the PMI Zambia chapter president, relates to that:

> Leading a team of volunteers is the most difficult task on earth, but the reward is learning to lead by inspiration and creating long-lasting relationships. You learn to build trust and not territories while accepting people's differences. This growth transcends self-actualization.

To develop this skill, you need to understand three fundamental principles:

- Don't assume volunteers are naturally motivated just because they volunteer.
- People are not robots. Their motivations fluctuate, and you may need strategies to remotivate them at times.
- Time spent now understanding your team's motivations is time gained in the future for your project.

Being a team leader is the best place to practice motivation. You need to build a sense of engagement with your team members. Take the time to understand their motivations and their purposes. Explain to them how they contribute to the global vision and purpose of the organization. And instilling a bit of fun will also keep people motivated.

These enriching experiences will equip you to motivate your team better at work.

TRANSFER TO YOUR PROJECT LEADER ROLE

It is essential to understand that there is not one motivational theory that fits all. You must try to understand what motivates your team now and tomorrow, and help your teams make a connection between what they are doing daily and how it serves a bigger goal and impacts their communities.

TABLE 3.1

Examples of Actions for Intrinsic Motivations

Intrinsic Motivation	Your Action
Learning	Articulate what they will learn from that project. Is training needed? Can they shadow other team members? Chat with their managers.
Increasing self-esteem	Give regular positive feedback about what they achieved and their strengths. Show them the progress made.
Collaborating	Propose they join a project where active collaboration is required.
Feeding curiosity	Send regular information about topics or training that may be of wider interest. Share information beyond the scope of the project.

As a project leader, you must plan regular check-ins with your team members to discuss their extrinsic and intrinsic motivations. For extrinsic motivations, you can advocate the managers of your team members for pay raises or promotions.

As far as the intrinsic motivations are concerned, Table 3.1 shows some examples of actions you can take.

It is not about inventing projects or tasks to harness your team members' intrinsic motivations. It is about helping them realize themselves and be happy.

You have mastered your communications, improved your collaboration, and demonstrated your ability to motivate your teams. However, unexpected situations can still arise. And you'll need to solve them.

IMPROVE YOUR PROBLEM-SOLVING

Understand the Benefits

Problem-solving refers to your ability to find a solution in novel or unexpected situations. It involves critical thinking, creativity, effective communication, and collaboration with others to overcome challenges and achieve desired results.

Let's step back for a minute. What if you are not keen to improve your problem-solving skills? What will you miss out on? If you cannot solve problems in your projects, they will quickly come to a halt. A project is a unique endeavor. You'll confront new situations, unforeseen changes, and unexpected issues. And you need to define the course of action to reach a goal.

Problem-solving does not mean finding complex and sophisticated solutions when the answer to the problem is simple. Effective problem-solving requires analyzing a situation, asking for help, and collaborating. You may follow a structured framework, like asking "why" five times. But sometimes, it doesn't work as expected, despite all you have planned and the risk mitigation solutions you have set up. Or perhaps you are faced with a problem that you cannot relate to your former experiences. That is where your problem-solving ability plays a significant role.

As a project leader, you need to develop this mandatory skill. By volunteering, you will confront novel situations and unexpected issues, because one thing is sure: you will have limited human and capital resources. This will force you to learn problem-solving.

Learn by Doing

Learning problem-solving skills is an ongoing process. You can gradually improve your abilities by consistently applying problem-solving techniques while volunteering without requiring substantial time investment. You can learn theories or use frameworks; you may already know some of those listed below. But the best approach is learning in the field and observing how people handle problems.

Practicing on a small scale and incorporating problem-solving into your routine will help you improve this skill.

Practice Problem-Solving

To enhance your problem-solving skills, you must be in the right mindset:

- Be curious about new solutions, even if yours are working.
- Accept that you may have to change the course of action, even if you have already planned everything.
- Be prepared to take on board lessons from diverse people, even if you are a competent project leader.

Before diving into concrete action, let's review how the American Society for Quality defines problem-solving. It is "the act of defining a problem; determining the cause of the problem; identifying, prioritizing, and selecting alternatives for a solution; and implementing a solution."[10] This is more than a definition: it provides a framework you may follow when you confront new problems:

- Define the right problem and involve the team.
- Determine the cause: a well-proved model is to ask "why" five times.
- Brainstorm alternative solutions. Gather information, talk with experts, and review the lessons learned.
- Select and prioritize solutions.
- Chart a course of action.
- Monitor the actions and adjust if necessary.
- Reflect on the process.

With this framework in mind, take the plunge! Choose an appropriate volunteer role to practice your problem-solving skills:

- Volunteer in some organizations promoting new projects or activities you have never been exposed to.
- Volunteering in events organizations or coordinating resources will provide a platform to practice problem-solving skills.
- Participate in online forums and discussions that promote critical thinking and problem-solving.

Sya, an active volunteer at the PMI Malaysia chapter, said:

> By volunteering, I've improved my problem-solving skills. I'm allowed to practice the lessons learned after making mistakes while volunteering. It's a good platform to learn from each other. There are challenges in volunteering, e.g., commitment, but with team building, practice, and knowledge, you can perform trial-and-error and practice solving the challenges that arise more easily. Then you can apply it in the working environment.

Transfer to Your Project Leader Role

Once you have developed strong problem-solving skills, you can become a better leader at work by applying them in the following situations:

- Decision-making: as a leader, you will face complex decisions that require analysis and problem-solving skills.
- Continuous improvement: a strong problem-solving mindset will help you continuously improve your day-to-day activities and organization processes.
- Strategic planning: applying your problem-solving skills allows you to develop robust strategies, create contingency plans, and swiftly navigate uncertainty.

Rashad Issa is an active volunteer mentor at the Chartered Quality Institute. His mentees bring issues and challenges from different sectors, and they provide some context for the problems they're facing. Rashad said:

> Of course, in mentorship, it's not up to me to resolve that issue, but it's having that conversation with them on how they would go about it, how they would manage their stakeholders, how they would use tools and techniques available in the industry to start analyzing and providing some solutions and seeing how professionals respond in different environments and sectors.

Engaging with mentees also helped him in his day job.

> My mentees have helped me see things from the point of view of my team members. I work with young professionals (young in experience); perhaps my team members are not bringing forward similar challenges. When I hear it from my mentees, I think: There is a challenge: how can I proactively remove such obstacles for my team?

Through problem-solving skills, you can build a strong foundation to address immediate concerns; however, to achieve long-term success you need to broaden your perspective – and strengthen your strategic thinking.

STRENGTHEN YOUR STRATEGIC THINKING

Understand the Benefits

Strategic thinking means looking carefully at situations, considering various factors and parameters, and devising a course of action. In other words, it involves planning and making decisions in a smart way that helps you or your organization achieve important goals.

Let's pause for a minute. What will you miss out on if you don't develop your strategic thinking skills? You may make wrong decisions that can have business, financial, and human impacts. You might think strategic thinking is just for executives. But every day, as a project leader, you must make the right decisions to deliver the best products and services that bring value to your customers. Strategic thinking is a significant skill to learn in this profession, regardless of your position in the hierarchy.

Use Models

Start by familiarizing yourself with strategic planning and thinking models, such as SWOT (Strengths, Weaknesses, Opportunities, and Threats) analysis, PESTEL (Political, Economic, Social, Technological, Environmental, and Legal)[11] analysis, and BSC (the balanced scorecard). These models help you zoom out on your projects.

SWOT analysis evaluates internal factors of the organization (strengths and weaknesses) and external factors (opportunities and threats).

PESTEL helps analyze the macro forces that an organization faces.

BSC measures four main aspects of a business: learning and growth, business processes, customers, and finance.

You can also read books and articles about strategic thinking. If you have a training budget, you can enroll in one of the many universities that offer online or in-person courses about strategic thinking, strategy development, and/or strategic planning. And, of course, you also learn by practicing.

How You Can Practice

When practicing your strategic thinking, you must acknowledge three things:

- Strategic thinking matters for every leader, regardless of their level and job title.
- Taking time to think before acting is not a sign of incompetence.
- Strategic thinking cannot predict the future.

Look for volunteer opportunities that allow you to practice strategic thinking. To do so:

- Seek diverse perspectives. Engage in international volunteer opportunities that expose you to different points of view, cultures, and backgrounds.
- Participate in a long-term planning session. Look to engage in a volunteer opportunity that allows you to create a strategic plan by setting clear goals for the position or volunteer role.
- Apply for a board position so that you can participate in the vision of the projectized organization.
- Ask strategic questions. For example, "Why are we doing this?", "What is the strategy behind these decisions?" or "How are the budgets created?" Doing this will allow you to exercise your communication skills and think more strategically, which will help you at work.

TRANSFER TO YOUR PROJECT LEADER ROLE

You have asked strategic questions in the volunteering setting; you have participated in strategic decisions. Now you can do the same at work. Here are some ways to develop your strategic thinking at work:

- Understand the big picture. Sometimes, as project leaders, we get caught in the weeds of the project. Understanding your organization's year goals and how your project contributes to them is essential to align efforts and priorities. You can look at existing information on a website or a strategic plan or ask your manager.
- Gather information. Your networking skills (which we will discuss later) will help you access the correct information that will nurture your decisions.
- Develop a project strategy and plans. When you understand the big picture and have all the relevant information, you and your team will be in a good position to develop possible plans.
- Use better tools and techniques. Learn and expand your toolkit, including things like risk analysis. This can help you make better-informed decisions and anticipate potential challenges.

CASE STUDY: HOW DO YOU MOTIVATE A TEAM OF VOLUNTEERS?

Samy* is a new project coordinator in the pharmaceutical industry. Outside of work, he would like to volunteer at a projectized organization in his industry.

After browsing the organization's website, he applied for a project leader role, organizing a face-to-face event in September, eight months away. During the interview, he learned he would work with Gertrud*, who was responsible for social media communication, and Milan*, the website administrator. The first thing he did was schedule one-on-one meetings with each of them to understand their roles and challenges.

During their conversation, Gertrud expressed demotivation due to team workflow issues. She faced challenges with delayed information and forgot to add the partner brand logo on the website. She had numerous innovative communication ideas, but they were consistently dismissed, and she struggled to obtain formal validation. Samy noticed her enthusiasm when she proposed creating a mini-video series. He inquired if she had communicated her challenges to the leadership. In response, Gertrud stated, with surprise, "I'm a volunteer. I don't have time to talk to people." Then Samy understood that she was seriously demotivated.

Samy approached Milan, the website administrator, to ask him to update the website. Milan acknowledged the request, responding, "I will do it." Because of the timeline, Samy inquired, "When?" Milan replied, "When I have time." As they continued their conversation, Samy realized that Milan wanted more recognition for his behind-the-scenes work.

These initial interactions overwhelmed Samy, making him question whether accepting the role as a volunteer team leader was the right decision, given the unexpected demand for more energy than he initially anticipated.

What should Samy do to keep Gertrud and Milan motivated?

Our Views

Leading a team of volunteers involves more leadership than a workplace role. You need to understand what drives your volunteer team. Some want recognition, and others want to learn new skills.

Samy spent time with Gertrud and Milan, asking direct questions and observing the nonverbal cues when they spoke. Samy realized that Gertrud wanted to set up a new video series. Samy should try to get approval from the management, even if just for an experimental period of, say, three months. This project could serve the organization and motivate Gertrud.

Samy noticed Milan wanted more recognition, so he must find ways to help. Perhaps Milan could be interviewed for the organization's newsletter. Or they could formally introduce Milan with a short biography on the website.

Understanding what drives the team takes time and effort, but it will pay off.

VOLUNTEERS' STORIES: AMERICO PINTO IN BRAZIL

Americo Pinto is the founder and chief executive officer (CEO) of PMO Global Alliance (PMOGA), later acquired by PMI. Since its creation in 2017, the organization has become the largest professional association dedicated to PMOs and PMO professionals globally. "Founding PMO Global Alliance and serving as its CEO has allowed me to put into practice the lessons I learned throughout my volunteer journey. The experiences and knowledge gained from volunteering have shaped my approach to leadership, strategy, and community-building within the organization," Americo told us. His volunteering journey began when he co-founded one of Brazil's first PMI chapters in 1999. At that time, he was already passionate about project management and saw the opportunity to contribute to the growth and development of the profession in his country. Since then, he has volunteered in various roles, from chapter leadership, event organization, speaking and presenting, and mentoring, to content development and global initiatives. For example, Americo led an international benchmarking study project for 11 years as a volunteer. Throughout this project, he collaborated with a diverse team and engaged with over 4,000 companies across 19 countries. This volunteer initiative enhanced his project management skills, such as coordinating a global team, managing stakeholders, and overseeing complex research processes. These activities have been profound learning experiences in different ways. "The credibility I gained in the team and community management field through volunteer work enhanced my professional reputation and expanded my network. It enabled me to connect with professionals who shared similar interests and challenges, further solidifying my credibility and establishing me as a trusted resource in the field," he told us.

Furthermore, the reputation he established through volunteering has been pivotal in gaining the trust and support of stakeholders within the industry. His worldwide recognition due to his volunteer contributions has provided a platform to advocate for the importance of PMOs and PMO professionals, shaping his professional journey and inspiring him to make a lasting impact in the global project management community. His firm, diverse, and international network of connections has proved to be instrumental in founding PMOGA. He added, "I had the privilege of building relationships with professionals from diverse backgrounds, cultures, and industries. These connections helped me gain insights into different perspectives and approaches to project management, expanding my knowledge and understanding of the field."

On the personal side, collaborating with professionals from different countries and cultures enriched his perspective and fostered connections with individuals he may not have otherwise met.

He has one regret:

> I wish I had known the immense impact volunteering would have on my life. Volunteering is not just about giving your time and skills; it is a transformative experience that enriches your soul, expands your horizons, and brings immense joy and fulfillment.

Thanks to volunteering, he stepped out of his comfort zone and embraced the opportunity to serve. He has discovered hidden strengths, forged lifelong friendships, and found a more profound sense of purpose.

Despite holding a leadership position, Americo still volunteers because he strongly believes in giving back and contributing to the community, which has supported his professional growth and success. More importantly, volunteering allows him to share his insights and help others navigate the challenges and opportunities in their own project management journeys. It will enable him to make a tangible difference by empowering others, elevating the profession, and fostering a collaborative and supportive community.

Americo cannot stop talking about the joy that volunteering has brought him. He gave us an essential last message for volunteers all over the world:

> The journey may have challenges, but the rewards are beyond measure. Embrace it wholeheartedly and be prepared to embark on an incredible voyage of personal growth, making a positive difference in the lives of others and leaving an indelible mark on the world.

KEY TAKEAWAYS

- Volunteering will help you practice and experiment with different leadership styles.
- Volunteering will help you improve your communication skills.
- Practice is essential for becoming a more collaborative leader.
- You will learn how to motivate teams.
- Volunteering enables the development of problem-solving skills across various contexts.
- You can improve your strategic thinking skills by using models and taking a step back.

YOUR A.H.A. MOMENT: ACTIVITY, HOPE, ACTION

It's your turn!

ACTIVITY

Answer the questions below:

- What is the leadership style that you use most? Why?
- Among the six leadership skills we've reviewed, what are two leadership skills you excel at? Why?
- What are two leadership skills you struggle with? Why?

HOPE

What leadership skills do you hope to improve by volunteering?
Prompt: "By volunteering, I hope to improve …"

ACTION

Write down an action you want to take in the next three months at work to practice one leadership skill (among the six) utilizing your volunteering experiences.

NOTES

1 PMI. (2023). Power Skills: Redefining Project Success. https://www.pmi.org/learning/thought-leadership/pulse/power-skills-redefining-project-success
2 Indeed Editorial Team. (2023, March 23). 18 Types of Leadership Assessments. https://www.indeed.com/career-advice/career-development/leadership-assessments
3 Stein, J. (n.d.). Using the Stages of Team Development. MIT Human Resources. https://hr.mit.edu/learning-topics/teams/articles/stages-development
4 Fenning, C. (2020). *The First Minute: How to Start Conversations That Get Results.* Alignment Group Ltd.
5 Grant, A. (2013). *Give and Take: A Revolutionary Approach to Success.* Viking; Manson, M. (2016). *The Subtle Art of Not Giving a Fuck: A Counterintuitive Approach to Living a Good Life.* Harper One; Marquet, L. D. (2013). *Turn the Ship around!: A True Story of Turning Followers into Leaders.* Portfolio; Sinek, S. (2017). *Find Your Why: A Practical Guide for Discovering Purpose for You and Your Team.* Portfolio; Sinek, S. (2019). *The Infinite Game.* Portfolio.
6 Herzberg, F., Mausner, B., & Snyderman, B.-C. (1959). *The Motivation to work* (2nd ed.). John Wiley & Sons.
7 Ryan, R. M., & Deci, E. L. (2000). Intrinsic and Extrinsic Motivations: Classic Definitions and New Directions. *Contemporary Educational Psychology,* 25(1), 54–67.
8 Pink, D. H. (2011). *Drive: The Surprising Truth about What Motivates Us.* Riverhead Books.
9 Michelman, P. (2007, August 30). The Three Signs of a Miserable Job. *Harvard Business Review.* Replace by: https://hbr.org/2007/08/the-three-signs-of-a-miserable
10 ASQ. (n.d.). Problem Solving. https://asq.org/quality-resources/problem-solving
11 Oxford College of Marketing Blog. (2016, June 30). What Is a PESTEL Analysis? https://blog.oxfordcollegeofmarketing.com/tag/pestel-analysis/#:~:text=A%20PESTEL%20analysis%20is%20an,%2C%20Technological%2C%20Environmental%20and%20Legal.

4 Enhance Your Adaptive Skills

One of the biggest challenges I've faced in volunteering is finding the courage to step outside my comfort zone. Yet, each leap has rewarded me with invaluable leadership skills and a community that fuels my professional growth and sense of belonging. Volunteering is a journey of discovery, development, and profound personal transformation for all of us!

Ricardo Viana Vargas
Global Leader in Project Management,
PMI Board of Directors Past Chairman

In this chapter, we will look at six challenges you are likely to face in volunteering, and in the workplace as well:

- managing organizational expectations
- managing your time
- managing your commitment level
- preventing burnout
- handling conflicts
- taming your ego

Thinking about each of these challenges, and allowing yourself to be exposed to them in a volunteer environment, can help you increase your immunity against them and help you confront them at work.

MANAGING ORGANIZATIONAL EXPECTATIONS

WHY IT IS IMPORTANT

In a new team and a new role as a volunteer, you must understand what is required from you regarding outcomes, quality, timelines, behavior, and reactivity. This comprehension will help you to align yourself with the team's objectives and prioritize your activities. When you clearly understand your role and activities, you can collaborate better and help meet organizational goals.

LOOK FOR CLARITY

When you join a new projectized organization and want to understand its expectations, you may think, "Let's ask other volunteers to find out what this organization requires." This seems like the obvious course of action, but it may not give you a definitive answer.

DOI: 10.1201/9781003407942-6

You may find that other volunteers are unable to give you a precise answer because they don't have a clear view, or different people may give you different answers, depending on their role and their place in the wider context of the organization.

Keeping this in mind, you can apply the following strategy:

- Gather information. Read the official description of your role, the organization's website, and the meeting minutes of its general assembly to find out its vision, mission, and strategy.
- Ask your manager, former volunteers, and the people who work with you. Consolidate this with your own initial experiences.
- Confirm your understanding with your manager based on the information you have gathered, and agree on expectations for the year.
- Create self-awareness. Reflect regularly on your performance, how you feel, and how your goals align with the organizational expectations.

TRANSFER TO YOUR PROJECT LEADER ROLE

Whether it's a risk assessment or a presentation you're working on, understanding how it fits with the company's goals is critical. Knowing the bigger picture will make your work easier and more enjoyable.

Raise questions to your colleagues, managers, or mentors at work to understand what is expected of you – and your team.

As a project leader, you also need to communicate the corporation's expectations to your teams. These expectations will shape their goals and form the basis for their performance reviews. Be aware that expectations can also change. Answer the team's questions honestly and adapt the goals accordingly. It will also help them to understand their priorities and to manage their time better.

MANAGING YOUR TIME

WHY IT IS IMPORTANT

Time management is planning and controlling how you spend your time. It also involves how you prioritize tasks and activities.

Time management is critical when you volunteer. As the workload fluctuates, or your availability changes, you can quickly become frustrated or disengaged with your volunteering activities. You want to enjoy the volunteer opportunity, learn leadership skills, expand your network, and try out new things. But to do these things, you must understand how to manage your time and fully grasp the time commitment required for your volunteer role.

Here are two ways to find out the time required from the outset of your engagement:

- Be sure to ask explicit and thorough questions about time commitment (we will give some examples in Chapter 10). This is volunteer work, not a second unpaid job.
- Be sure it will fit your personal, professional, and family life and will not generate frustration or stress.

No matter how enthusiastic you are about your volunteer role, you must learn to turn off your computer sometimes and set boundaries whenever possible. Volunteering doesn't need to take up all your free time or impact your family or work schedule. A few hours per week can offer you some of the benefits you seek. When volunteering, you need to feel that it is fun and rewarding. You need to enjoy it: it should not become just another item on your "to do" list.

But this is easier said than done, due to several factors:

- Temptations for continuous engagement: you would like to excel in your role.
- Emotional investment: your passion and dedication make you emotionally invested in the role or your assigned task.
- Perception of your own importance: you may feel your continuous involvement is crucial for success.

There may be times when setting boundaries is difficult, and you may sometimes feel obliged to work in the evening and at the weekend. But still, it is essential to maintain a healthy balance.

ANALYZE YOUR SITUATION

You need to consider three primary parameters:

- your work and family commitments
- your availability and flexibility
- the task workload

Work and Family Commitments

First, review your work and family commitments. Then determine how many hours you can commit to the volunteer opportunity and whether it fits the organization's requirements.

Availability and Flexibility

Remember to check if the volunteer opportunity you are interested in has mandatory meetings and, if so, when and where they are held.

Now that you have thought about these issues, write down your availability (including commuting time, if needed) and the time you will need to commit. That will give you a fair time commitment assessment. Compare this with the number of hours officially required by the volunteer role.

Can you make it work? Are you willing to do a bit more or not?

Think about these two situations:

Situation 1: Jon* wants to volunteer for a projectized organization; however, he only has two hours available on Wednesday afternoons. Jon should look for a flexible volunteer opportunity that can be completed in the available time.

Situation 2: Amelia* is interested in a virtual volunteering role, but one that still involves close relationships with teams; however, she can only volunteer early in the morning (around 4 a.m. local time). Amelia should look for global opportunities in a different time zone from where she is located.

These two examples show how important it is to understand time commitments and how you can find solutions to challenges by simply reflecting on the practical details of the situation.

Task Workload

The last parameter, the task workload, is the trickiest one. If the activity is not new, ask how long it typically took for former volunteers and the challenges they faced; if they are still in the organization, you can ask them about this yourself. You also need to factor in the time needed to acquire new knowledge. Will you work alone?

Delegation is another way to improve time management. If the activity is new, you can't rely on existing data on time management, but you need to predict how much it will take, based on your experience or by talking with experts.

The good news is that you can apply the same techniques to improve your time management at work.

Transfer to Your Project Leader Role

Time management is always raised as one of the main issues at work.[1] When we interviewed volunteers for this book, we were surprised to find they highlighted an unexpected beneficial outcome of their volunteering activities: they learned to manage time, prioritize, and focus because they had to find time to work *and* volunteer.

Time management depends on workload, priorities, delegation, interest, and competence. It is essential to master it at the project, professional, and personal levels:

- Project level: time management will help you prioritize tasks to achieve your goals.
- Professional level: when you organize your time efficiently, you can deliver more things and carve out some time to learn or experiment. It will also reduce your stress.
- Personal level: it will give you a better work–life balance and time for more extra-professional activities.

You can do a simple time-management exercise: track the time you spend on each task for a few weeks. You may find out how to optimize your time. You can also timebox your activities. For example, allocate one hour to work on a particular presentation or 30 minutes to review a specific document. You may discover you get distracted easily (30 minutes can easily turn into an hour). Another method to manage your working time is the Pomodoro technique[2]:

1. Pick a task.
2. Focus on work for 25 minutes.
3. Take a break of 5 minutes.
4. Repeat four times and then take a more extended break of 15–20 minutes.

So, learning and improving in the volunteering sandbox will allow you to learn how to balance multiple priorities and meet your project due dates. Paying attention to time management will also help you to detect decreases in your level of commitment.

MANAGING YOUR COMMITMENT LEVEL

LACK OF COMMITMENT IMPACTS THE PROJECT

You have just joined a new team. You and your peers are excited about the project ahead.

For the first few days, everything is golden; however, something happens at work or in your personal life. Then you drift away, and nobody takes care of your designated task.

Regardless of whether this happens to you, or another team member, the outcome is the same: the situation will create an extra workload for someone else.

During your volunteer engagement, keep an eye out for the warning signs of declining commitment and monitor your engagement level. Lack of commitment is not just a one-off missed deadline; you also need to look out for recurring issues such as frequently missing meetings, failure to complete work, or a negative attitude, all of which can indicate a decline in your overall engagement.

Nhung Nguyen, an event director at the PMI Vietnam chapter, loves volunteering but honestly acknowledges the reality of the challenges involved: "Volunteering is real hard work and also requires commitment. It might not be your priority, but it is time-consuming and energy-draining, and you have a target to achieve."

FIND OUT THE ROOT CAUSES OF YOUR LACK OF COMMITMENT

If you want to improve your lack of commitment, you must be honest with yourself. You need to identify the root causes of the problem.

If it is a workload issue, ask for a longer timeframe or talk with people who performed the activity before and ask them how long it took them. That will not give you all the answers, however, because people may do things differently, the contexts might have changed, and the team and their engagement depend on the personal relationships that have been built, that is, how well they know each other. Think about whether you have performed this kind of task before; this will give you a general idea of the workload.

Another possible cause of decreasing commitment is that you may have been asked to carry out an activity or implement a change at very short notice, and you don't like it in the volunteering setting. Is this a recurring issue? Talk with your volunteer manager about the expectations of that role to understand if you fit or not.

If you think your lack of commitment is a competence issue, find out whether you can have a mentor or training.

Now that you understand how to improve (or help a team member improve), be honest with yourself or the team member. If you are the one who cannot commit, be transparent and direct with the team, explain the reasons, and step down. They will appreciate your honesty. If you observe a team member's lack of commitment, you will have an opportunity to have an honest, challenging conversation and discuss with them how you can help with it.

Here are two situations that show how the root causes of declining commitment can be analyzed:

Situation 1: Ryan*, a project event planner, consistently struggles with executing specific aspects of event planning. His portfolio manager suspects a competence gap. To identify the root cause, she organizes a skills assessment session. She then provides training opportunities to address any identified gaps in Ryan's competence.

Situation 2: Liz*, a volunteer in charge of web design, feels disengaged when assigned last-minute design changes. Suspecting that short notice might be the issue, she schedules a team meeting to address workload distribution concerns and ensure everyone has adequate time for task completion.

The great news is that when you have practiced all these things in your volunteer role, you can take what you have learned into your project leadership role!

Transfer to Your Project Leader Role

It's crucial to understand that a lack of commitment will have a root cause: personal issues, dissatisfaction with the role, or a mismatch between the role description and day-to-day activities. You will be monitoring yourself and understanding why you aren't committed, and you will be able to explain the situation to your managers.

On the other hand, if you observe a lack of commitment from team members, you will be ready to analyze the root cause and have a difficult conversation with them to find solutions and support them. It doesn't matter how tricky the situation is; the volunteer laboratory was the perfect place to practice and you will have learned how to be honest with yourself or your team members at work.

A combination of inadequate time management and a lack of commitment can result in burnout.

PREVENTING BURNOUT

Why It Is Important

The World Health Organization (WHO) has defined burnout at work as "a syndrome conceptualized as resulting from chronic workplace stress that has not been successfully managed."[3] This definition was based on the extensive research of Christina Maslach, emerita professor of Psychology at the University of California, Berkeley, and expert on workplace burnout.

In their book *The Burnout Challenge*, Christina Maslach and Michael P. Leiter have identified "six forms of mismatch" between a job and a worker, which can result in burnout:

- work overload
- lack of control
- insufficient rewards
- breakdown of communities

- absence of fairness
- value conflicts[4]

Some of these forms of mismatch can occur in the volunteering setting. In other words, burnout also happens to volunteers. That's why it's essential to recognize the warning signs.

How to Detect and Address Burnout

First, you need to confirm if you are stressed or burned out. Stress can be relieved if the situation improves. Burnout is the consequence of chronic work-related stress: you feel exhausted and hopeless, and you don't find any meaning in what you're doing. Let's review two situations:

Situation 1: Anna* is usually engaged, participates in all the meetings, and volunteers for tasks outside her role. During the last few months, she has seemed demotivated, skipped meetings, and is doing the bare minimum. If you observe this behavior with Anna, you should schedule a one-on-one meeting to understand why she is less engaged than before. Prepare the conversation in advance. Ask open-ended questions and listen actively.

Situation 2: A month ago, Jose* took up a new volunteer role in technology. He observed that some other volunteers in the finance, governance, and communication teams weren't doing their tasks. He started doing other teams' tasks alone. He soon felt tired, and then overwhelmed by his own and other people's tasks. He decided to leave.

Instead of quitting because he was burned out, Jose should have communicated his concerns to the leadership team. Requesting support can avoid burnout.

Maisa Husain, a volunteer in Bahrain, gives insightful advice:

> In my experience, volunteering is vital to expand your horizon beyond your work routine and advance your professional skills. But one must also treat any volunteer opportunity as a project, not an ongoing program. One should define one's level of volunteering and limits. Always choose the kind of volunteering opportunities with a defined deadline ... Many volunteers run into a cycle of volunteering with no deadlines or targets, and become exhausted after a while, which may, sadly, make them regret the idea of volunteering.

Can volunteering actually *prevent* workplace burnout? A study about general volunteering found that pediatric nurses who volunteered at a camp for children with cancer were more resilient against workplace burnout, thanks to the coping skills they gained through volunteering.[5] This resilience was partly due to their deeper personal connections with their patients, which added to their professional and unique sense of purpose.

Yasmina volunteered at a time when she experienced a high level of stress at work and dissatisfaction. Through volunteering, she could make an impact in the community, which helped relieve her work-related stress. In our conversations with volunteers, some also pointed out that volunteering helped alleviate their work-related stress. Volunteering helps people find other purposes outside of work and regain their humanity. They can close their work laptop and open their personal laptop to connect with the volunteering world. It gives them that extra adrenaline rush.

Transfer to Your Project Leader Role

As we have explained, burnout results from chronic work stress. If you think you are suffering from burnout, it could impact your team members and they may need support as well.

But you may not be a psychologist or an expert in the field. Your workplace may provide some training about detecting and handling burnout. But if you feel that professional help is needed, don't wait. Enquire about the official paths for raising the issue of burnout at work. There might be a human resources manager, a workplace doctor or nurse, or a confidential helpline to call.

Volunteering is rewarding and fulfilling, but as a team member you must also know how to handle conflicts.

HANDLING CONFLICTS

The Importance of Addressing Conflicts

A conflict is a serious disagreement between two or more people. Some people are convinced it is better to avoid or ignore conflict. However, most of the time, a conflict is not solved by itself. Unresolved conflicts can lead to more significant issues: people don't talk about their conflicts and will have difficulties collaborating in the future. That's why, as a project leader, you must learn to address team conflicts.

How to Improve Your Conflict-Handling Skills

When dealing with conflict, the first step is to determine its root causes. Here are three common causes of conflicts in teams:

- lack of clarity in roles
- silo working
- personality clashes

Lack of Clarity in Roles

In one of our volunteers' surveys, we asked: "What do you wish you had known about volunteering?" One of the respondents answered, "Better understanding of the role and responsibilities. Ambiguity is part of volunteer roles and may have impacts."

Digging deeper, we realized that not all organizations provide detailed role descriptions for volunteers. An incomplete role description can cause conflict in different ways:

Situation 1: We leap into work without knowing the boundaries, we overstep, and we tread on other people's toes.

Situation 2: We don't deliver something and are a roadblock for other volunteers because we don't know we need to perform a particular task.

If the organization does provide a role description, we recommend reviewing it and asking questions about any flaws you see in the description before committing.

If you can see ways in which the role description can be enhanced, this is a valuable observation, perhaps even indicating that your experience could support the organization's governance. You can help draft and review your role description and challenge the team members to develop a more precise role description in line with what is really expected.

Silo Working

Volunteers sometimes work in silos. They may not be aware of the other members' tasks and what they are doing. Here are two examples:

Situation 1: At EmpowerPM Network*, silos emerge between the social media team and the professional development team. These two teams don't work together or communicate. The social media team promotes events from other organizations and not the events of EmpowerPM Network itself, leading to low attendance numbers. This silo approach results in missed opportunities to maximize participation in their own organization and support for the organization's events.

Situation 2: At QualityPM Foundation*, the sponsorship team promised a sponsor that their logo would be bigger than those of other sponsors on the website. However, the web team discovered that the website's design didn't support adding logos of different sizes. The technical constraints prevented them from fulfilling the sponsorship team's commitment.

To effectively break the silos, we recommend reviewing the communication between teams, ensuring that everyone knows each team member's activities. Check also the organizational processes in place. If people work in silos, perhaps they are following poorly designed procedures. If you observe any issues of this nature, you should review and redesign the process.

You can also foster a collaborative culture where everyone can reach out for help; you can start by being an example and reach out publicly to your colleagues when you need assistance.

Personality Clashes

Different personalities may cause varying expectations, disagreements, and conflicts. Almost everyone has some inflexible personality traits that could lead to clashes if not appropriately managed. Some team members may focus on interpersonal differences rather than the organization's goals.

Personality conflicts pose a significant challenge in organizations with high volunteer turnover. Personality conflicts can arise during volunteer opportunities because of differences in communication style, approaches to work, work ethics, and competing priorities, among other things. Here are a couple of examples of personality clashes:

Situation 1: Santosh* is an introvert. He works daily with Anita*, an extrovert; their different personality traits lead to misunderstandings in communication and collaboration.

Situation 2: Laura* is direct in her communications. She clashes with Sarah*, who prefers a more indirect communication approach. Their personality and communication styles lead to tensions during team meetings.

Both situations involve communication challenges due to differences in personality traits and communication styles in the workplace. If you experience situations similar to these, we recommend exploring communication training or workshops. Create a work environment where each team member can share their thoughts by setting ground rules and setting aside dedicated time to talk; finally, schedule follow-up sessions with the impacted team members to provide constructive feedback.

TRANSFER TO YOUR PROJECT LEADER ROLE

When you have learned how to handle and solve conflicts during your volunteer roles, you will be ready to be a better project leader. Learning how to clarify or explain your volunteer role to others will help you at work when you need to write a role description for your upcoming hire. You'll be aware of the emergence of silos, and you will be ready to create a strategy to break them up if they emerge.

Regardless of the source of the conflicts, you need to set some ground rules for yourself and your team:

- Use "I" messages (instead of "you") and concentrate on facts while expressing your feelings and your perceptions.
- Talk about your needs.
- Let the other party say their piece.

While these rules are important, remember that their specific application may change depending on the nature of the conflict, the individuals involved, and your organizational culture. Hence, we always recommend monitoring and controlling the conflict and setting a follow-up to adapt the resolution in the future if needed.

TAMING YOUR EGO

WHY IT IS IMPORTANT

Volunteering gives you access to many people and industries. You may get the important title you dream of having in the workplace (and you don't). It nurtures your ego. You may seek personal visibility to the detriment of the team's visibility. You go to events. You are photographed with famous or influential people in the project management world, and you are tagged on social media. It may give you a feeling of power. And you may want to take part in more events and not share the spotlight with your team.

HOW TO KEEP YOUR EGO IN CHECK

An overinflated ego is something that anyone can experience, regardless of their position or circumstances. Here is our advice for avoiding it:

- Clarify your motivations for volunteering (we will explain in detail later).
- Review the goals of the organization.
- Review your role description.
- Understand why your ego has become a problem.

Let us review two situations:

Situation 1: You want to be seen everywhere. If you have fallen into this trap, you must remind yourself of the purpose of volunteering. Project volunteering is not an individual role. It is a teamwork role and is intended to empower the team. You can volunteer in order to gain social exposure, but not for this reason alone. As a leader, if you see a peer displaying an overinflated ego, you need to understand the expectations of this person and tactfully manage them by clarifying their role's objectives.

Situation 2: You may feel you want to be informed of everything, and involved in everything, even if it lies outside your role. Perhaps you love advising and helping, even if no one asks you to do so. In this case, maybe you could become a mentor or lead a mentorship team.

Transfer to Your Project Leader Role

At work, people can display their ego in different ways:

- Mona* always wants to be the one to present to top management and does not give credit to the team.
- Yul* only talks about his projects at work.

How can these situations be managed? First, you should acknowledge the contributions of each individual to the project's success.

As a project leader, you are also responsible for being a "good" role model for your team. Lead by example. You need to be the one who praises your team and gives credit to their hard work and engagement. When you are around other project managers, don't just discuss your own "big project." Listen to others, their initiatives, and their challenges. This will give you a greater understanding of other projects in the organization.

Develop a supportive network that can give honest feedback about how you behave and the impact on your team. It will help you manage yourself and keep your feet on the ground.

CASE STUDY: AM I A COMMODITY?

Vega* has volunteered for a few months as a moderator for webinars. He is independent in his volunteering role, which he likes. In the past, he helped to arrange his organization's annual gathering, which was exhausting, because it involved back-to-back meetings. At least in this new volunteer role as a webinar moderator, he is happy.

One day, five minutes before a webinar is due to start, he gets a new script about what he is supposed to say as an introduction to the webinar. He is surprised because he has been moderating the webinars for a while and this has not previously happened. As it is short, he does not complain and follows the script. The speaker had also sent a new photo three days before the webinar, but again Vega is only informed at the last minute, and he has to rush to change the visuals in the slides. On another occasion, he is informed that a webinar has been canceled only two days before the event.

Are his knowledge and experience not recognized by his organization? His motivation to work with them is being undermined. People should have kept him posted about what was going on and let him know in good time about any changes. He feels like an object that people use when they need it, rather than a valued contributor.

What should Vega do?

OUR VIEWS

Vega should raise the issue with his manager and redefine how information is communicated between teams. He should define a RACI (responsible, accountable, consulted, informed) matrix with the roles and responsibilities to clarify his remit. Then, he can apply this for future webinars.

VOLUNTEERS' STORIES: RUTH PEARCE IN THE USA

Ruth Pearce, the founder of a coaching and training company, is a committed volunteer; she has truly enjoyed her journey of giving back to her community. Ruth has taken on multiple activities and responsibilities throughout her various volunteer roles. From engaging with residents and staff at a nursing home to organizing and coordinating events, she has tirelessly devoted her time and attention to those in need.

Ruth's journey began when she received a humble request from someone she deeply admired and trusted, sparking her desire to make a positive difference. "Volunteering reminds me of who I am and where I came from," Ruth reflects, drawing inspiration from her parents, who nurtured in her the values of generosity and service.

Volunteering has not only allowed her to forge meaningful connections but has also served as a platform for networking, especially when venturing into new organizations. Ruth told us she has unforgettable memories of her experiences at conferences, where she enthusiastically handled the registration desk, seizing the opportunity to engage with diverse individuals.

Ruth has developed a course about Project Burnout, so we took advantage of her expertise and asked her about burnout in the volunteering setting.[6] Ruth emphasizes the importance of recognizing the signs of burnout and setting realistic expectations for one's volunteer work. "It's crucial to assess the amount of time and energy you can devote to volunteering to make a meaningful impact without overwhelming yourself," she advises.

However, Ruth admits that the commitment and workload often exceeded her initial expectations, leading to moments of burnout. She encourages volunteers to prioritize self-care, establish boundaries, and communicate their needs effectively to avoid overwhelming themselves. "It's important to listen to your well-being and not hesitate to seek support when needed," Ruth emphasizes.

Maintaining a delicate balance between work, personal life, and volunteering has been a significant challenge for Ruth. As a self-employed individual, she must distinguish between volunteer work and paid work. Ruth has learned not to overcommit herself by focusing on one organization at a time, as it helps prevent conflicts arising from time and energy constraints. Moreover, she ensures that her colleagues and clients know and support her volunteer work, allowing for flexibility when necessary.

And it's OK to stop volunteering. According to Ruth, when you feel resentment or are undervalued in the volunteer organization, it's time to have a break.

Another sign is when you have too much on your plate.

While she occasionally takes breaks from volunteering to concentrate on special projects, like writing her book, Ruth acknowledges the intrinsic satisfaction she derives from volunteering, drawing her back time and again.

Ruth remains an advocate for the power of giving back. She actively encourages others to explore volunteer opportunities aligned with their passions and interests, urging them to recognize the signs of burnout and prioritize self-care in their journey.

KEY TAKEAWAYS

- When volunteering, you'll have to manage expectations, time, and commitment levels. Being honest with yourself and others provides a solid basis for achieving this.
- Volunteering will expose you to different kinds of conflicts. Take the opportunity to practice conflict management strategies and resolutions that you can apply in your work.
- Don't assume that excess workload is the only cause of burnout. Dig deeper to find the root cause.
- During your volunteer journey, you will encounter people who are only there to feed their egos; don't be one of them! Maintain your own values and work hard to ensure the success of the organization that you are volunteering for.

YOUR A.H.A. MOMENT: ACTIVITY, HOPE, ACTION

It's your turn!

ACTIVITY

Answer the questions below:

- What are the two challenges (among the ones discussed in this chapter) you've faced most often in your volunteer role?
- How did you overcome them?
- How did the projectized organization help you to overcome them?

HOPE

What adaptive skill do you hope to manage better?

Prompt: "By volunteering, I hope to manage better…"

ACTION

Write down one action you want to take in the next three months to improve one adaptive skill.

NOTES

1 Timeular. (2023, December 18). Time Management Statistics You Need to Know in 2024. https://timeular.com/blog/time-management-statistics/
2 Collins, B. (2020, March 3). The Pomodoro Technique Explained. *Forbes.* https://www.forbes.com/sites/bryancollinseurope/2020/03/03/the-pomodoro-technique/
3 World Health Organization. (2019, May 28). Burn-out an "Occupational Phenomenon". *International Classification of Diseases.* https://www.who.int/mental_health/evidence/burn-out/en/
4 Maslach, C., & Leiter, M. P. (2022). *The Burnout Challenge: Managing People's Relationships with Their Jobs.* Harvard University Press.
5 Butterworth, L., Nasr, A., Pyke-Grimm, K. A., Swisher, D., & Johnson, K. (2021). The Impact of Volunteering at a Family Camp for Children and Adolescents with Cancer: The Experience of Pediatric Intensive Care Nurses. *Journal of Nursing Administration*, 51(10), 526–531. https://doi.org/10.1097/NNA.0000000000001058
6 Pearce, R. (2022). Project Manager Burnout: Recognizing, Disrupting, and Reversing. LinkedIn Learning Course. https://www.linkedin.com/learning/project-manager-burnout-recognizing-disrupting-and-reversing

5 Develop Your Network

[T]he currency of real networking is not greed but generosity.[1]

Keith Ferrazzi and Tahl Raz
Authors of Never Eat Alone

Many books have been written about networking. However, in this chapter, we want to show you how volunteering helps you develop your network exponentially to learn, make friends, and eventually benefit your current and future jobs. You'll be able to audit how your network operates. Gorick Ng, a bestselling author and a Harvard career advisor, will share insights on how volunteering can be instrumental for people from low-income and underrepresented backgrounds.

UNDERSTAND THE BENEFITS

Growing your network through volunteering allows you to exchange knowledge and ideas, discover new opportunities, and build valuable relationships locally or globally that can turn into friendships. It is essential for personal and professional development.

On the personal side, social interactions foster a sense of purpose and well-being.[2]

On the professional side, volunteering will help you expand and diversify your network. You will have access to new circles of relationships in other industries and sectors you are not connected with through your daily jobs. You will work with people with different academic and socioeconomic backgrounds, work and life experiences, positions in the professional hierarchy, ages, cultures, countries, nationalities, religions, genders, gender expressions, and sexual orientations. You will hone your communication skills as you collaborate on multiple projects. You may even find your next gig. Jennifer Fondrevay, executive coach and global speaker, told us:

> My volunteering activities in the speaking club have enabled me to connect more deeply with other speakers. And for speaking, referrals from other speakers can be a great source of business. I didn't do it for that reason, but it has been a welcome outcome.

Whether it is on the personal or professional side, you can gain a lot from networking in a volunteering setting. You may find a new accountability buddy, a role model, a mentor, or a friend. You will remain open-minded to new knowledge that you may not have accessed otherwise. More importantly, networking can be instrumental in your career and life. Ahmed Zouhair, president of a consulting and training firm, has told us, "Volunteering has helped me meet some of the great people that helped guide me in the right direction and also kept me out of trouble as a young professional." This happens because networking is less daunting when you volunteer.

DOI: 10.1201/9781003407942-7

THE EASINESS OF VOLUNTEER NETWORKING

In the workplace, networking may be more transactional because of the business environment. Furthermore, networking at work may have some roadblocks that impede you from expressing yourself freely or asking questions. First, you may feel that you are risking your credibility and reputation when you network at work. You may wonder, "What are others thinking of me?" "Is this a silly question to ask?" Second, it can be intimidating. You are part of a workplace hierarchy that can present barriers to networking. For instance, you may think, "I cannot talk to this top manager because we are not at the same level." On the contrary, networking in volunteer opportunities is more accessible because everyone is there with the same willingness to support a cause. You can collaborate with a bank manager, a software company CEO, or a chief marketing officer.

You will learn networking on the ground.

NETWORKING CAN TAKE DIFFERENT FORMS

Would you like to improve online or face-to-face networking? Would you like to introduce yourself in an impactful way? Or do you want to know the basics of small talk?

Networking is a skill you can learn and develop.[3] Some individuals excel at it, and others need more practice. You may be convinced you are not gifted at it. But it's important to realize that networking can take different forms. Putting people in contact with each other, sharing your expertise, and sending a relevant article to colleagues are all forms of networking. We will help you with concrete advice later in this chapter to leverage these different forms.

You can read books and participate in courses or webinars on the subject, but there are also practical ways to learn. Identify people who are clearly good at networking and ask them to mentor you. Or you can observe the actions of an expert networker you know during a face-to-face event.

You are going to meet many people by volunteering. You're going to have the chance to talk with them. Seize every opportunity to practice these forms of networking.

PRACTICE NETWORKING BY VOLUNTEERING

To network effectively, you must have the right mindset:

- Be convinced you have exciting things to share.
- View networking as a way to discover new knowledge through human connections.
- Remember that networking may lead to new business, employment, and skills growth opportunities.

The first thing that you should practice is building rapport. Imagine that you are attending a conference. First, check to see if the participants' list is available on the website or in a mobile application dedicated to the event. Check their social media to find commonalities and connect with them before the live conference.

When you arrive in the meeting room, you'll feel like you are meeting old friends if you have already talked with them before the conference. If they tell you important information about themselves, write it down. For example, when someone tells you, "I have an important presentation to come," make a note of it; then, when you meet them, you can ask how it went.

Then, practice how you will introduce yourself to other people, in a way that fits the event. Refrain from improvising, even if you are self-confident. In his book *The Serendipity Mindset*, Christian Busch suggests casting hooks: mention a job, a passion, an interest, and a hobby.[4] Doing this creates a greater likelihood that you will find common topics to discuss – and ultimately bond.

During the conference, you should approach each person with an open and non-judgmental mindset. For example, you can tell yourself, "I commit to being open to the people I am going to meet today and I will see what I can learn." Recall what they spoke about if you had any communications with them before the meeting.

During the conversation, practice active listening and be aware of your body language. Don't look around the room for famous influencers while talking with someone, and don't look at your watch if the person speaking doesn't interest you.

What if you are networking online? The same rules apply. Introduce yourself briefly and leave space for others to do the same. Maintain eye contact when you talk, and look at your camera, not your computer screen.

By following these steps, you can overcome your fear of small talk – and enjoy the conversation.

TRANSFER TO YOUR PROJECT LEADER ROLE

If you only associate networking with business cards and business development, it's time to reframe it. Networking is building relationships (and business cards are a tool, not the aim). We want to give you some practical tips to help you improve your networking skills easily and enjoyably. For this, we will draw on some research literature.

Monica L. Forrest and Thomas W. Dougherty have identified five dimensions of networking behavior for managers and professionals:

- maintaining contacts
- socializing
- engaging in professional activities
- participating in the community
- increasing internal visibility[5]

Let us review each dimension in turn.

MAINTAINING CONTACTS

Maintaining contacts (and remembering people's names and which industries they work in) is a crucial skill for a project leader. When you meet people, check their social media profiles after the meeting and associate some keywords with their names.

Here are some other actions you can take:

- Exchange business cards or QR codes at face-to-face events.
- Send "I'm thinking of you" notes with relevant information for your contacts. For instance, whenever you read an article, listen to a podcast, or watch a YouTube video, you can send them a note like "I thought of you when I came across this article/podcast/video that might interest you." You can keep "in loose touch."[6]
- Put people in contact with each other.
- Meet online or for lunch.

SOCIALIZING

Socializing includes introducing yourself, participating in small talk, concluding a conversation, and following up. Remember that you don't need to improve all aspects of your socializing simultaneously; start small so as not to be overwhelmed.

Here is how to do it:

- Participate in work social events.
- Reconnect with former friends.
- Take on extra work activities with colleagues.
- Talk about personal activities at work.
- Prepare a catalog of stories related to your main skills so that you can take part in spontaneous conversations and highlight your strengths.

ENGAGING IN PROFESSIONAL ACTIVITIES

You can become a better project leader by getting out of your comfort zone, going beyond the frontiers of your job description, and giving back to professional projectized organizations.

Here is how to do it:

- Write blogs or articles for professional journals, professional associations, or internal websites.
- Present a webinar or apply to speak at conferences.
- Attend an event or a conference.
- Volunteer, of course!

PARTICIPATING IN THE COMMUNITY[7]

You can also give back to your communities. This is a way to expand and diversify your network.

Here is how to do it:

- Lead or participate in a project in your community.
- Attend meetings or social events in your community.

TABLE 5.1
Self-Assess Your Networking

Form of Networking	Level of Proficiency (0 = none, 5 = optimal)
Maintaining contacts	
Socializing	
Engaging in professional activities	
Participating in the community	
Increasing internal visibility	

INCREASING INTERNAL VISIBILITY

Don't think that your achievements will speak for themselves. Take intentional steps to shine. After all, you deserve it.

Here is how to do it:

- Have lunch with your bosses.
- Say hello individually to your coworkers.
- Take on highly visible work or tasks.

SELF-ASSESS YOUR NETWORKING

Use Table 5.1 to assess your level of proficiency in each form of networking (on a scale from 0 to 5).

Your self-assessment will show you which aspects of your networking abilities need to be reinforced, and you can use it to develop an action plan.

NETWORKING FOR YOUR CURRENT AND FUTURE JOB

Networking in a volunteer setting can help you in your current and potential future job.

CURRENT JOB

If you join local volunteer groups, a community of practice, or a community of experts, you will get to know other people in your field. The first advantage of this is the chance to enrich your knowledge: you can learn new ways of working, discover new tools, or find out about forthcoming disruptions. You can also create a support network to solve problems or clarify doubts. And if you are part of communities within your corporations, they can also be a source of knowledge about forthcoming changes in your company – or new job opportunities.

FUTURE JOB

You can create genuine relationships that transform into future paid employment when you network in your volunteer roles and meet new people. You can talk informally with people about what they are doing, and people may share more about their jobs outside of their daily tasks. Mac Prichard, a recruitment and career expert, encourages people to volunteer when they are job hunting because volunteering is an opportunity to prove what they can do. It is also a chance to talk informally with people in their field. And this is a way to access the hidden job market and to be aware of forthcoming jobs. But he highlights an important point:

> You should always, as when volunteering, give your time and energy with the expectation of receiving nothing in return. And if you start with that mindset, you will be amazed at what you get back in return when you do so without expecting anything.

Networking can play a particularly significant role for people of low-income and underrepresented backgrounds, as we discovered when we interviewed Gorick Ng.

INTERVIEW WITH GORICK NG: NETWORKING FOR PEOPLE FROM LOW-INCOME BACKGROUNDS

Gorick Ng, a *Wall Street Journal* bestselling author of *The Unspoken Rules* and a Harvard career advisor, shares his views on this topic.[8]

a. *Based on your experiences, how does volunteering play a role in helping people of low-income and underrepresented backgrounds to rise to positions of leadership?*

It would be best if you were seen, heard, and known to rise to leadership positions. You need someone higher up to see who you are, remember what you want, and bang on the table for you to be picked over someone else. Few positions in the workplace – especially at the junior level – give you this level of visibility. Volunteering gives you a chance to break beyond your day job in a way that putting your head down and working hard never can.

b. *What benefits of volunteering can you highlight for people of low-income and underrepresented backgrounds?*

Volunteering for cross-team projects, committees, employee resource groups, or community service efforts is a great way to develop your skills and knowledge; build valuable relationships; and establish a track record of going above and beyond. You get to add resume bullet points you would otherwise not be able to add, learn unspoken rules you would have otherwise not known about, and meet people you would otherwise not be able to meet. For someone of a low-income or underrepresented background, this knowledge and these networks could mean the difference between getting that promotion – or even knowing that you could get promoted – and not.

c. *A more personal question: how has volunteering helped you in your career? Please share some examples/stories.*

Some of the most valuable professional relationships are ones that I built by volunteering. Had I not volunteered for a student leadership initiative in high school, I would have never met a mentor who ended up showing me the unspoken rules of applying to college. Had I not volunteered for a political campaign in university, I would have never learned how the system works – and not have talking points for job interviews. Had I not volunteered to help train a new hire at work, I would have never been able to demonstrate my leadership skills – ones that my manager wrote about in a future reference letter. Few opportunities I've been fortunate to have have come to my doorstep. They came as the result of me raising my hand.

CASE STUDY: HOW DO I EXPAND MY NETWORK BY VOLUNTEERING?

Hikaru* has just begun to volunteer on the membership team of a projectized organization.

His task is well defined: he has to analyze the database and regularly present statistics visually to the board of directors and the president of the projectized organization. He has learned much about database management, which will benefit him at work.

His manager made the presentation for the first meeting, and Hikaru observed. At the next meeting, he will be the one to present. To prepare his presentation, he is in contact with many volunteers in the organization. He must also understand the current needs and gaps to give an overview of the situation. But during each exchange with them, he goes straight to the point and sticks to the agenda. He doesn't take the time to talk with them. Occasionally there are in-person events for volunteers, but he does not attend those. Before the next presentation, his manager has proposed having lunch with the organization's president.

Hikaru hesitates. He doesn't talk much and thinks he will talk even less in front of the president.

Should Hikaru accept?

Our Views

Yes, he should accept. He has a unique opportunity to be introduced to the organization's president. He can then find out more about the organization's strategy. Hikaru must also try to carve out time to get to know some volunteers, even if it involves getting out of his comfort zone.

Expanding your network begins with seizing every opportunity.

VOLUNTEERS' STORIES: PRIYA PATRA IN INDIA

Priya Patra never thought of the impact she would make when she began volunteering in 2015. Priya is a program manager in an Information Technology (IT) services organization in India. Before volunteering, she had two misconceptions about it: "I thought you needed to have a lot of time to volunteer, and you needed to be a retired person to be a board member." She began to take on some short-term assignments to give her a taste of volunteering. For example, she was a conference paper reviewer for the PMI India chapter national conference. She was impressed by the wealth of knowledge she gathered from that assignment. It encouraged her to contribute to projectmanagement.com. She also presented at PMI conferences. "It's always an amazing experience of learning, connecting, and networking," she told us, with a big smile. Since then, she has taken on many roles as a volunteer: a reviewer and subject matter expert, an advocate for volunteers, speaker roles at many international conferences, and a PMI chapter board member. She has also founded a women's community – Women PowerUP Network – a global virtual community of around 800 women spanning North America, Latin America, Europe, and Asia. "We are not a business but a community with a purpose to our vision – empower with the right support and skill to transform the future. Right now, we are providing a platform to enhance leadership qualities."

Through her extensive speaking engagements, Priya gained confidence in sharing Agile knowledge at work and at international conferences.

Volunteering has also been an opportunity for her to lead global initiatives. For example, the PMI Chapter Xchange initiative involves an international team representing more than 22 nationalities. They organize events and share knowledge between PMI chapters. And she has even written a book about this experience with her team colleagues.

Thanks to this initiative, Priya was able to improve her cultural agility and transfer it to work. She is now more at ease working with a remote, culturally diverse team. She has led global work initiatives with confidence, like rolling out a competency development program organization-wide across regions. She was also able to hone other leadership skills, for example, influencing without authority. Leading volunteer teams is very different from leading project teams at work. "Remember that volunteering projects are not regular corporate projects. Volunteers must be constantly motivated and see value propositions in the projects." It has helped her articulate the value proposition for any project she leads to keep her team motivated.

Since she began volunteering, she has never looked back. "I am a true proponent of the word 'Volunesia', meaning: a moment when you forget that you're volunteering to help change lives because it's changing yours." Volunteering for her is all about learning, cross-pollinating ideas between her work and volunteer projects, and networking.

Priya recommends keeping an open mind, connecting with people from diverse backgrounds, and learning from them – it really makes a difference.

She concluded: "Volunteering has truly helped me become a much better leader at work. Volunteering has changed my life for sure and can change yours. Don't miss the opportunity, hop in and create an impact!"

KEY TAKEAWAYS

- Networking in volunteer environments involves lower stakes than at work.
- Networking has different forms; it involves maintaining contacts, socializing, engaging in professional activities, participating in communities, and increasing visibility.
- Cultivating networking opportunities through volunteering can ramp up your professional career.

YOUR A.H.A. MOMENT: ACTIVITY, HOPE, ACTION

It's your turn!

ACTIVITY

Answer the questions below:

- What benefits do you find in networking in a volunteering setting?
- What form of networking have you mastered best?
- What form of networking do you most need to improve?

HOPE

How do you hope to grow your network?
  Prompt: "I hope to grow my network by …"

ACTION

Write down an action you want to take to grow your network in the next three months.

NOTES

1 Ferrazzi, K., & Raz, T. (2004). *Never Eat Alone, Expanded and Updated: And Other Secrets to Success, One Relationship at a Time.* Random House.
2 The Royal Society. (2004). The Social Context of Well-being. *Philosophical Transactions of the Royal Society B: Biological Sciences*, 359(1449), 1435–1446. https://doi.org/10.1098/rstb.2004.1522
3 Boitnott, J. (2019, June 11). Effective Networking Requires Mastering These 5 Skills. *Entrepreneur Magazine.* https://www.entrepreneur.com/starting-a-business/effective-networking-requires-mastering-these-5-skills/335014
4 Busch, C. (2020). *The Serendipity Mindset: The Art and Science of Creating Good Luck.* Riverhead Books.
5 Forrest, M. L., & Dougherty, T. W. (2001). Correlates of Networking Behavior for Managerial and Professional Employees. *Group and Organization Management*, 26, 283–311.
6 Wickre, K. (2019). *Taking the Work Out of Networking: An Introvert's Guide to Making Connections That Count.* Gallery Books.
7 The factor defined in the research was "Participate in church and community," but we decided to make it more inclusive.
8 Ng, G. (2021). *The Unspoken Rules: Secrets to Starting Your Career Off Right.* Harvard Business Review Press.

6 Explore New Fields

Volunteering is the crucible in which we forge problem-solving prowess, cultivate expansive networks, and establish unassailable credibility in uncharted domains. It imparts the art of transforming challenges into opportunities, masterfully weaving a web of connections, and elevating individuals into trusted authorities in their chosen fields.

Dr Darius Danesh
CEO – Australian Institute of Project Management

This chapter will help you explore new fields to future-proof your career and professional development. You will learn to:

- experiment with new things to help you go beyond your limits
- remain curious and be open to novelty
- gain credibility in new fields as a result

EXPERIMENT WITH NEW THINGS

UNDERSTAND THE BENEFITS

Simply put, experimenting with new things means trying things out: this can include tasks, activities, projects, or responsibilities, whether in your field of expertise or not. Within your own field of expertise, you can use new tools, technology, or ways of doing things. Take Laure-Emmanuelle, a web administrator in her day job. One day, she was contacted to help as a volunteer for the web administration of a not-for-profit. She accepted and said, "It is easier as this is my strong suit. I can test new things without the work pressure."

You can also venture outside your field of expertise; for instance, if you are a technical project leader in your day job, you can volunteer in the marketing team.

And what if you don't experiment with new things? What will you miss out on? You may entrench yourself in your own field of expertise and become less open to new ways of working or new knowledge. You may not get used to developing learning strategies or new problem-solving techniques and become less adaptable. The numerous changes in the world, in organizations, and in ways of working force you to react, adjust, and adapt even if you don't want to.

When you experiment with new things, you become used to developing your learning agility.[1] You nurture your creativity and remain curious (more about this later in this chapter). And lastly, experimenting with new things will help you to know yourself better by discovering new strengths, new drivers of motivation, or new purposes at work and in life.

DOI: 10.1201/9781003407942-8

How You Can Learn

Skills and abilities are not set in stone, and your existing field of expertise does not define you as a leader or as a human being. Cultivate a growth mindset, so that you can regard the chance to try new things as a learning opportunity.[2] With a growth mindset, you can develop your skills with hard work, good strategies, and help from others.

In a volunteer setting, there are different ways that you can learn and experiment with new things; you can engage in activities that allow hands-on experience, where you can familiarize yourself with a new system, a new tool, or best practices. Volunteering often offers a supportive environment where you can express your creativity, try new ideas or approaches, and be the best version of yourself.

How You Can Practice

To facilitate your experiments, first, you must accept three principles:

- You don't know everything.
- You have to take risks.
- You can make mistakes; it does not indicate a failure of your technical competence or leadership abilities.[3]

Second, identify your main motivations for experimenting with new things. These could be:

- You do not have opportunities to try new things at work.
- You do have these opportunities, but you don't have the confidence to seize them in the work environment.
- You don't currently need the skills you'll gain by experimenting, but you will require these skills for a future work position.

Last, be honest with yourself.

Do you like trying new things, being challenged, and starting from scratch? Then, you'll be delighted to choose volunteer roles in new domains. Failures will not stop you from moving forward.

Or do you need a safety net? Do you need a mentor to guide you, or do you need to shadow someone first? Start by sticking to your field of expertise. Ask the volunteer team if there is some written documentation on how to perform the role, the processes and stakeholders involved, and the lessons learned. Once you gain confidence, you can try new things unrelated to your workplace expertise; enquire if you can be mentored by an expert in the domain who can support you in your learning journey, or if there is some training you can take.

Whatever your mindset, select what you want to experiment with by completing the sentence below:

"As a leader at work, I want to *learn/improve/become proficient in A*. In the volunteering setting, I will *choose that activity to practice A*."

Example:

"As a leader at work, I want to *improve the visual presentation of the slides.* In the volunteering setting, I will *volunteer in the communication team to produce slides for webinars.*"

Here is a short list of criteria you can use to choose the best volunteer role for experimenting with new things:

- What do you want to get out of your experiments?
- What are the challenges you are ready to face?
- What are the risks you are happy to take?

As soon as you can, apply what you have learned at work.

TRANSFER TO YOUR PROJECT LEADER ROLE

Assess your work environment. First, answer the following questions to evaluate the level of experimentation allowed in your organization:

- How much wiggle room do you have to go outside of your remit or job description?
- How are mistakes treated?
- How are new ideas handled in the organization?

The following questions will evaluate your ability to experiment with new things at work:

- How often do you go beyond your role?
- How do you feel when you say, "I do not know"?
- What level of vulnerability do you allow yourself?

For You

When you volunteer in your own field of expertise, you may apply your new learning at work. If you have discovered a new tool that helps you be more efficient, you can propose it at work if it is authorized. If not, perhaps you will be inspired to look for an equivalent tool that is allowed. You may be convinced you can't introduce new things into your work environment, but we are not talking about major revolutions here. You can do small experiments. For example, you may see that an existing process works well, but perhaps there are some ways to optimize it.

If you volunteer in a completely new domain, you may transfer your learning now or in the longer term. If you design visuals for social media in your volunteer role, you may become more interested in improving your corporate presentations. Little by little, you will gain confidence in things you would never imagine you could master.

For Your Team

Beyond your new learning and the self-confidence you have gained, volunteering will also give you ideas for creating an environment where experimenting with new things is possible. When you and your team confront something new, reframe it in a positive way: "We're going to use this new tool as an experiment and reflect on the lessons learned." It will calm the minds of your team, empower them to participate in the changes, and enhance their creativity.

Research has shown that the conditions that undermine creativity in work environments are:

- constraints in carrying out tasks
- lack of freedom
- surveillance
- competition
- focusing on extrinsic motivators[4]

Think about each of these conditions; identify the ones that most frequently create roadblocks in your workplace and, if you can, set up strategies to counter them. For instance, to counter a lack of freedom, you can give your team more free space and time to let them explore new ideas. You can "normalize" mistakes and reframe them as lessons learned. You will not necessarily change your corporation overnight, but you can contribute to creating an environment where curiosity flourishes.

REMAIN CURIOUS

CURIOSITY AMPLIFIES YOUR SKILLS AND NETWORKS

Curiosity can be seen as a personal quality that has nothing to do with business and the workplace. But what if you aren't curious at work? What will you miss out on? You may turn your back on new skills (because they are not required for your role), new contacts (because you don't have common ground), or new knowledge (because you don't need it now).

If you are not curious, you can unintentionally limit your horizons. According to one source, "The average half-life of skills is now less than five years; in some tech fields, it's as low as two and a half years."[5] With this pace of change, you need to build a strategy to access new knowledge and develop new skills so that you can adapt. And this can be achieved by deliberately confronting new situations. Volunteering can contribute to this.

LEARN BY DELIBERATELY CONFRONTING NEW SITUATIONS

How can you do this? You can do it through communities and personal discipline.

You need to be intentional to get in contact with new people who will be your source of knowledge. As we explained earlier, when you grow your network, you increase your opportunities to remain curious and discover new people and things.

The best thing to start with is to engage in communities where diversity is fostered, because you can find different perspectives and viewpoints. But how do you know if the community encourages diversity? Check the participants, their backgrounds, and their history. Also check the level of engagement in the community. Are people's questions answered? Do the answers help? Are diverse thoughts respected or is groupthink more common? If you can't figure out the situation, contact community members to learn more.

Also check the ground rules: does the community encourage live conversations? Don't limit yourself to project management communities. For example, Yasmina is part of a marketing and coaching community, things that do not have direct links with her day-to-day job. She felt out of place when she first joined the marketing community, as there were many things she didn't understand. But looking back, it helped her to meet music producers, best-selling book authors, and executive coaches, which increased her networking agility.

Personal discipline can also help you.

Mauro Guillén, professor of management and vice dean at the Wharton School at the University of Pennsylvania, recommends having a systematic strategy for learning new things[6]:

> Every night … I read an article about … a topic that I know very little about. So lately, … I'm doing this on archaeology. And it's really enriching me. It's really helping me see connections that I would never actually detect if I didn't do that.

You can also take an online course about curiosity, like the one developed by the behavioral scientist and management expert Francesca Gino.[7] But the best way is to practice.

Seize Every Opportunity to Practice Curiosity

To remain curious, you need to accept three principles:

- Human relationships are a lively source of knowledge and learning.
- Asking questions is not a sign of incompetence.
- Exploring other interests and areas is not a waste of time.

Volunteering is your practice laboratory, because it gives you countless opportunities to meet new people and discover new fields.

If you go to a conference, perhaps an Indian colleague will mention cricket, a sport that is widely loved in India. You may have no interest in cricket (and that's OK), but you should ask some questions about it. By doing so, you are learning something new and creating a deeper connection with this person. Maybe you can connect more genuinely and talk more easily to your Indian colleagues or anyone who loves cricket in the future. You are increasing your small-talk capital, another source of forging genuine relationships.

Next time you are tempted to say "No" to an unexpected email, request, or video call, refrain; and instead think, "Let's see what I can learn." You never know where it can lead you. That is what happened to Rosa Gilsanz, a project manager in the oil and gas industry in Germany. She began her volunteering journey at the PMI Germany chapter in the women's group of the diversity circle. Then, the opportunity came to submit a topic for the annual chapter conference:

> I thought that it was a great opportunity to contribute with our personal experience as female project managers, boosting discussion on the situation of female project managers and making an impact. This time, the audience would be the whole project manager community in Germany attending the conference. I wasn't looking for the opportunity to present at a face-to-face conference. But when the opportunity came, I seized it.

The panel discussion she collaborated with was a success. And it all began with just a spontaneous idea! – and a curious mindset.

TRANSFER TO YOUR PROJECT LEADER ROLE

What you have practiced in the volunteering field can be translated into work, for you as a project leader, and for your teams to bolster their curiosity:

- Allow yourself to experiment with new things, as we discussed earlier in this chapter.
- Develop learning habits.
- Engage in genuine conversations by asking questions and listening properly.

For You

Carve out time to learn regularly about topics not directly related to your field.

Questions are a powerful tool when you interact with people. But asking questions is not enough: you must listen to the answer beyond the usual small talk. You can discover a new idea to explore. During meetings, you can also ask questions you feel the team doesn't dare to verbalize. Asking questions (and admitting your ignorance) will also model a safe psychological environment for your team members and encourage them to do the same.

For Your Team

At the team management level, curiosity can be an intrinsic motivation for some of your team members. Here are some ways to nurture their curiosity:

- Give them a variety of different activities.
- Introduce them to new people they wouldn't otherwise have opportunities to meet.
- Review whether they need training.
- Encourage their managers to allow them time for exploration.

When people are solely focused on progressing through their to-do lists, they don't have time to ask questions or the energy for new activities. Allowing your team members time and space to maintain a sense of wonder will promote creativity and innovation.[8] And you'll help them to gain credibility in new fields.

GAIN CREDIBILITY IN A NEW FIELD

UNDERSTAND THE BENEFITS

Gaining credibility in a new field means expanding your repertoire of skills. "New fields" can have different meanings:

- New areas: for example, if you work in technology and want to move to healthcare.
- New products or technologies: for example, if you work in telecoms with product A and want to move to product B.

In the latter case, the path is easier.

You may want to gain credibility in a new field for many different reasons. You may be curious to learn more without a precise agenda. You may be preparing yourself for the future with no concrete plan. You may want to diversify your knowledge to move into a new role. Or you may want to change careers.

But we must be clear. Gaining credibility through volunteering does not automatically mean a new job or a career change. In some countries, qualifications and work experience are more important than extra-professional activities (more on this in Chapter 7). Nevertheless, it is still worthwhile to increase your credibility in several different ways, and volunteering is one useful option for this.

Why is it important? You will probably not have the same job or work in the same firm your whole life. You may become a project leader in a new domain you don't know much about. Learning to gain credibility will push you to be attuned to coming trends and, as a result, to remain employable (we will talk about this in Chapter 7).

One thing is sure: volunteering can play a role by broadening your skillset, and you'll learn to gain confidence in new domains.

HOW YOU CAN LEARN

Consider Monica*, an engineer. She volunteered in marketing and communication. She discovered a real passion for marketing, and she resigned from her job. She decided to launch her own small marketing services agency, something she would only have thought about after volunteering. She discovered new interests and reinvented her career.

Answer these questions to devise a learning strategy:

- Are you hoping to enter a new industry, or take up a new role? Choose a volunteer organization in this industry or a role related to what you want to learn.
- Are there recognized certifications in this field? Are there professional bodies where you can volunteer?
- Is there training you can take or recommended books to read? Talk with people who already work in this new domain.

When you volunteer, you can have discussions (or "informational interviews") with people in that field, firm, or industry.[9] Ask them to describe how they got to where they are, the skills they needed, and the challenges they faced. Theoretical knowledge and conversations will not be sufficient, however; you also need to learn on the ground.

Overcome Impostor Syndrome

To gain credibility in a new field, you need to accept three principles:

- It takes time and effort.
- You need to surround yourself with a supportive network.
- Impostor syndrome is part of the journey.

Impostor syndrome is defined in the *Merriam-Webster Dictionary* as "a psychological condition that is characterized by persistent doubt concerning one's abilities or accomplishments accompanied by the fear of being exposed as a fraud despite evidence of one's ongoing success."[10]

If you suffer from impostor syndrome, you may think, "I'm not qualified for this role," or "Why should I even try it?" But as we explained earlier, you will gain confidence by experimenting with new things in a volunteering setting where the stakes are less high than at work. And it will encourage you to be bolder in your job.

Barend Daniel Peters, IPMA-South Africa president, acknowledges that volunteers sometimes need clarification on the value they can bring: "There's always a little bit of self-doubt, but if you start acting on things, things start moving forward. Then things keep building onto each other, and before you realize it, people value your work."

You can transfer this value to your project leader role.

Transfer to Your Project Leader Role

Thanks to volunteering, you can change your mindset about how to reskill (learn a new type of work) and gain confidence in unfamiliar environments. Having a supportive network, experimenting, and remaining curious are the ingredients for your success.

For You

If you have to lead projects in a new area, take this three-step approach:

- Have discussions with project leaders and experts in that field. After each interview, write down in a journal their lessons learned and their challenges.
- Enquire about the necessary certifications or theoretical knowledge (books, newsletters, professional bodies).
- Look for relevant training.

For Your Team

It is your responsibility to help your team members grow as project leaders and develop their careers. In one-to-one conversations, listen to the doubts that prevent them from moving forward and look for solutions to remove the roadblocks. Again, the three-step approach is useful:

- Introduce them to people or communities who can give them more information.
- Encourage them to acquire certifications.
- Advise them to look for relevant training.

That is what Annesha Ahmed, business strategist and board volunteer at the PMI Bangladesh chapter, highlights:

> Volunteering opens up many opportunities for learning new things, meeting new people, and refurbishing the thought process. Suffering from impostor syndrome is unavoidable and part of the learning journey. But it is so rewarding. For example, these priceless volunteering experiences taught me to hone my soft skills when working with young minds, which I could use at work with my diverse team.

By volunteering, you can go beyond your limits, which contributes to your employability.

CASE STUDY: YOU DON'T HAVE ANY MARKETING BACKGROUND. WHY ARE YOU A VOLUNTEER IN A MARKETING TEAM?

Fred* is an IT specialist and has several project management certifications. He applied for a marketing role in a projectized organization. To Fred, as an IT special-ist, this was an excellent opportunity to expand his knowledge to a new domain. Many of his colleagues at work had moved from IT to marketing. He was not inter-ested in marketing, but he thought, "Why not try it in a volunteer role? There is no risk if I have a competent mentor I can learn from."

He was responsible for designing a marketing strategy to promote events. He had many ideas. He took a short training course in marketing. In the volunteer organiza-tion, he began to hear some comments behind his back: "Fred is not knowledgeable about marketing. Why is he in the marketing team?" or "I don't understand why he is volunteering in marketing with no marketing background." His new confidence in marketing began to falter.

Should Fred go on volunteering in the marketing team or choose to volunteer in the IT team instead?

Our Views

In some countries, academic background defines a person's credibility almost for life. In other countries, people trust and admire the willingness to try out new things. What is the culture of the country where Fred lives?

Another critical point is that a marketing expert mentors Fred. Before Fred takes on the marketing role, he can shadow a marketing expert to understand what is required. Then, during his tenure, Fred can contact the marketing expert with any questions. The marketing expert will be available to answer Fred's questions to guide him. Volunteering doesn't mean you can do a terrible job because you are on the learning curve.

Fred could move to the IT team to use his expertise, but we recommend he stays on the marketing team as this is one of the benefits of volunteering, as we have seen: the chance to experiment with new things. As leaders and volunteers, we should encourage and develop the mindset and behaviors of our volunteer peers so they can go out of their comfort zone.

VOLUNTEERS' STORIES: JONATHAN LEE IN SINGAPORE

"Being able to have a meaningful, positive impact on the community in my youth ignited my passion for volunteering, and I have not looked back since. It has led me to subsequent opportunities over the past two decades. And I look forward to further opportunities ahead of me," said Jonathan Lee.

Jonathan does business development and account management at work and is a passionate volunteer and board member in various Singaporean institutions and associations, including the PMI Singapore chapter, where he is a vice president. "Volunteering has been a source of personal fulfillment and growth, providing a platform to apply and enhance my skills in real-world scenarios beyond the professional realm. This personal growth has positively influenced various aspects of my life, fostering a sense of purpose and fulfillment in making a positive impact," he told us. First, volunteering helped him build meaningful and lasting connections beyond his professional industry. He had the joy of collaborating with project managers worldwide who shared common values and passions, contributing to a sense of community and shared purpose. "This is a huge advantage in terms of gaining new perspectives for similar challenges one could face at work (e.g. managing stakeholders, applying new methodologies, understanding potential challenges, etc.)."

But these connections have also enriched his life, providing a supportive network beyond the workplace boundaries. "I love the sheer exposure to diverse people in myriad industries, which inspires me to open my mind to different experiences from similarly passionate people," he added. Thanks to his volunteer experiences at PMI, he has learned how project managers in other industries, such as construction, technology, pharmaceuticals, and the public sector, address similar challenges but often differently. To him, it is an invaluable, eye-opening human experience no book can replace.

Furthermore, it has enhanced his credibility as a leader and contributor to the project management community. Indeed, his various leadership roles have allowed him to demonstrate his ability to adapt to unpredictability and influence people of different backgrounds, skills, and personalities across different situations. In one of the associations where he volunteered, in his capacity as the lead director of an international conference he had to influence a group of close to 100 volunteers recruited across different countries and drive them towards clear objectives in a time-boxed manner. "This required effective delegation across portfolios (e.g. sponsorship, finance, senior stakeholder relations), which allowed me to distinguish myself in future work roles," he said.

Volunteering has given him two invaluable gems: communication and collabora-tion. "Strong communication builds trust and ensures everyone is aligned, making navigating challenges easier and inspiring a collaborative and motivated team."

Volunteering forces people to interact with peers who possess a variety of motiva-tions, often with competing priorities. "This is something I am fortunate to have been able to demonstrate at work when additional responsibilities outside my job scope come my way and also when I am required to engage with external stakeholder orga-nizations for tangential initiatives (e.g., Corporate Social Responsibilities, Marketing Events, etc.)," he told us.

Throughout his volunteer journey, he has learned to effectively negotiate with senior stakeholders, which has helped him become comfortable with building rela-tionships in his current role in business development/account management.

These connections made, skills developed, and lessons learned in the volunteer arena have been powerful catalysts for his personal growth and career advancement. He has become a better, well-rounded project manager, enhancing his professional reputation – and employability. "Ultimately, the journey of volunteering is a continu-ous cycle of learning, giving, and receiving. It's a testament to the interconnectedness of professional and personal development and well-being. It paves the way for posi-tive change within oneself and the communities served," he concluded.

KEY TAKEAWAYS

- By volunteering, you can experiment with new things that are not part of your day job.
- It helps you remain curious and open to new skills, new people, and new ways of doing things.
- By practicing in the volunteer setting, you'll overcome impostor syndrome and gain credibility in new fields that you can transfer to work.

YOUR A.H.A. MOMENT: ACTIVITY, HOPE, ACTION

It's your turn!

ACTIVITY

Answer the questions below:

- With what new things would you like to experiment by volunteering?
- How do you remain curious?
- In what fields would you like to gain credibility?

HOPE

What do you hope to overcome by exploring new fields?
Prompt: "I hope that by exploring new fields, I will overcome…"

ACTION

Write down an action you want to take to explore new fields in the next three months.

NOTES

1 Valcour, M. (2015, December 31). 4 Ways to Become a Better Learner. *Harvard Business Review.* https://hbr.org/2015/12/4-ways-to-become-a-better-learner
2 Dweck, C. (2007). *Mindset: The New Psychology of Success.* Random House Publishing Group.
3 Keating, L. A., Heslin, P. A., & Ashford, S. (2017, August 10). Good Leaders Are Good Learners. *Harvard Business Review.* https://hbr.org/2017/08/good-leaders-are-good-learners
4 Amabile, T. M. (2020, July 6). How Your Work Environment Influences Your Creativity. *Greater Good Magazine.* https://greatergood.berkeley.edu/article/item/how_your_work_environment_influences_your_creativity#:~:text=Our%20studies%20revealed%20that%20intrinsic,and%20not%20by%20extrinsic%20motivators
5 Tamayo, J., Doumi, L., Goel, S., Kovács-Ondrejkovic, O., & Sadun, R. (2023, September–October). Reskilling in the Age of AI: Five New Paradigms for Leaders – and Employees. *Harvard Business Review Magazine.* https://hbr.org/2023/09/reskilling-in-the-age-of-ai
6 Coaching for Leaders podcast, Episode 642: How Generational Learning and Working Is Changing, with Mauro Guillén. https://coachingforleaders.com/podcast/generational-learning-working-changing-mauro-guillen/
7 Gino, F. (2022). Leverage the Power of Curiosity at Work. LinkedIn Learning Course. https://www.linkedin.com/learning/leverage-the-power-of-curiosity-at-work-to-adapt-and-grow-with-francesca-gino
8 Gino, F. (2018, September–October). The Business Case for Curiosity. *Harvard Business Review Magazine.* https://hbr.org/2018/09/the-business-case-for-curiosity
9 Heine, A. (2023, June 10). A Complete Guide to Informational Interviews (With Benefits). Indeed.com. https://www.indeed.com/career-advice/interviewing/informational-interview-guide
10 Merriam-Webster. (n.d.). Impostor Syndrome. Merriam-Webster.com dictionary. https://www.merriam-webster.com/dictionary/impostor%20syndrome

7 Remain Employable

What you may not directly get to do at work for career achievement and passion, you can get to do as a volunteer. Volunteering allows you direct opportunities to participate in varied boundless initiatives, to expand your knowledge and experience, to develop your skills, to give back and to do much more!

Ike Nwankwo
Programme Management Consultant, PMI Board of Directors

So far, you have learned that by taking advantage of volunteer activities, you will develop new skills, network, and explore new things, and as a consequence, you will remain employable. In this chapter, a university professor, Manuel Souto-Otero, will help you understand the link between volunteering and employability. Then, you will discover how volunteering can help you remain employable in four specific situations:

- You are unemployed.
- You are self-employed.
- You work in corporations.
- You are transitioning from military to civilian life. To support this part of the chapter, we interviewed Joe Pusz, one of the founders of the Veteran Project Manager Mentor Alliance (VPMMA).

Rosabeth Moss Kanter, a professor at Harvard Business School, was one of the first scholars to draw attention to employability. She defined it as "a person's accumulation of human and social capital – skills, reputation, and connections – which can be invested in new opportunities that arise inside and outside the employee's current organization."[1]

We talked with Manuel Souto-Otero, DPhil in Social Policy from the University of Oxford, to dive deep into this. His main areas of interest are education policy analysis and evaluation, especially the link between education and work (including, although not restricted to, digitalization, the future of work, and its implications for skills development).

INTERVIEW WITH MANUEL SOUTO-OTERO: VOLUNTEERING, EMPLOYABILITY, AND LEADERSHIP

a. *What is the link between volunteering and employability? How does volunteering help workers to be more employable? Does it only benefit young professionals?*

Volunteering helps workers become more employable by developing people's skills, particularly soft skills, and can also help build technical skills. It can also help show a good fit with a company, for example, or other

DOI: 10.1201/9781003407942-9

organizations that may provide employment. It does not only benefit young professionals; it benefits people at different stages of their working lives. Now, people who are in the early stages of their careers may find it particularly useful to undertake volunteering to complement other experiences and help them show that they possess specific knowledge, skills, competencies, attitudes, etc. that they cannot show so much, perhaps, through their professional experience.

b. *Does volunteering only benefit knowledge workers' employability?*

Volunteering benefits knowledge workers' employability and the employability of workers at very different levels on the occupational scale. You can volunteer to undertake an enormously wide range of tasks, some of which may be basic and others very advanced. As I mentioned, it can also show certain attitudes and values that employers may consider and value in recruitment processes. Those attitudes and values may be positively regarded in some employment positions that are very high in the occupational hierarchy but also in the middle or at the bottom of the labor market.

c. *What role does volunteering play in acquiring soft skills? For example, if you have a technical background or are a project leader?*

Volunteering helps develop a wide range of soft skills. We see an increasing demand for hybrid profiles in the labor market. These profiles combine both technical and soft skills. So, even with a solid technical background, you may still need advanced soft skills ... Those soft skills may include communication, emotional intelligence, adaptability, leadership, creativity, time management, problem-solving, teamwork, and project management. These are all skills you can develop through volunteering, where you will work with others in your organization and other organizations with a social purpose to achieve common goals. You may also engage directly with beneficiaries, helping you develop this skill. Now, this sort of skill may be developed to a different extent. For example, volunteering is often associated with developing emotional intelligence and empathy as you try to understand other people's perspectives. These people may be experiencing hardship or an otherwise challenging situation. Another soft skill often associated with volunteering is time management, as many volunteers volunteer part-time and combine their volunteering work with paid work. Since third-sector organizations often have limited resources, as a volunteer, you may need to develop your creative thinking and skills as you approach other organizations or individuals for help. These are just some examples of soft skills often perceived to be developed through volunteering.

d. *How can volunteering help you change your career?*

We have already discussed one way in which volunteering can change your career. You may be able to develop your skills or gain new experiences in ways that help you advance your career. But there are other ways in which volunteering may help you change your career. You can also get to know new people and develop your network. That network may help you find new work opportunities you would not otherwise have discovered. Finally, through volunteering, you may find a new vocation and decide to change your occupation or the sector where you work. It may be related to more than just working in the third sector. You may try a new role during your volunteering experience that makes you rethink your career goals and objectives and change the course of your career. It can help you develop, reimagine, or reinvent yourself.

e. *How can volunteering help you become a better leader?*

Volunteering can help build leadership skills. It may allow you to set up or lead a team. It can also help you develop your empathy with others; it can help you become a more compassionate or socially responsible leader. It may make you a leader who understands other populations or market segments (and people in your team) in ways that you would not have understood in the same way if you did not have volunteering experiences. You may also become a leader who values diversity and inclusion to a greater extent (these are hot topics for many organizations in the public and private sectors today) and a better-networked leader.

FOUR EMPLOYMENT SITUATIONS

Now, let's focus on four employment situations in which you may find yourself and how volunteering can help you in these circumstances.

You Are Unemployed

When you are looking for a job, you can sometimes feel discouraged and lose self-confidence in your abilities and work experience. Volunteer your expertise "to remind you that you have skills."[2] It will boost your self-esteem because your competencies and experience are needed and valued. And you can keep abreast of trends and necessary skills.

The other direct benefit is to fill a gap in your CV. But don't do it just for that reason. Put your heart into it. Another advantage of volunteering, if you are unemployed, is the natural social connections that arise. When you are unemployed, you may feel too shy to contact people: perhaps you feel embarrassed because you don't have a job (since many people define themselves by their jobs), or you got out of the habit of interacting with people, or you don't think you have any topics to talk about.

When you volunteer, you will work within an organization along with other volunteers. Your genuine passion for helping can even lead you to find a job in a volunteer organization. Dorie Clark features Becky Last in her book *The Long Game*.[3] Becky had been volunteering for six months as a technical advisor to the Ministry of Tourism in Vanuatu when a cyclone struck the Pacific Island nation. As part of the recovery efforts, she worked in close partnership with teams from the World Bank Group, which later resulted in a consultancy position and, ultimately, a staff role. Although Becky's story is an exceptional one, it is nevertheless true that volunteering will pave your way for future jobs, not just in the organization where you volunteer. As we saw in Chapter 5, you can access a hidden job market. Your new volunteer friends may be keen to share your CV with their firms or contacts.

The last main advantage is reinventing your career. Being unemployed can force you to think about your career as a project leader.

Some project management organizations offer specific projects for unemployed people. For example, Leap to Success, a nonprofit in Austin, Texas, provides job seekers with pro bono projects with a 4- to 6-week timeframe.[4]

You Are Self-Employed

If you are self-employed, maintaining continuous leadership development might become challenging because you are unable to benefit from corporate training. You may have an irregular income and be cautious about how much you invest in your professional development. If you are in this situation, volunteering provides a way to help you develop skills without investing much money in training.

Volunteering also gives you an exclusive learning platform, allowing you to access hands-on leadership training and network opportunities that will drive your career forward.

Sometimes, as a self-employed person, you may work alone. By volunteering, you will be able to boost your leadership and collaborative skills.

Lastly, you can find future business opportunities through the network you establish from volunteering. But engage genuinely and ethically. You may have access to databases for partners. Engage with them for the organization's benefit, not just for your own purposes.

You Are Employed in Corporations

If you work in a corporation, you will usually have access to a learning platform, and you probably have a professional network already. Why would you be interested in volunteering?

First, as discussed earlier, volunteering can help you sharpen your leadership skills and experiment with new things you cannot try at work. Second, you'll be able to expand your existing network and cultivate authentic relationships to help you put the stress of your day job into perspective.

On the psychological side, volunteering can provide a safety net for your corporate life. In our surveys, some volunteers commented that they could cope with corporate life because they found meaningful ways to impact their community outside their corporations. For others, it was a way to break up corporate life's monotony and lack of challenges.

Be cautious about time management if you commit yourself to volunteer activities. You have obligations to your employers first. We also recommend checking your contract and employee covenants to find out whether you need to inform your employer about your volunteer role and whether your firm's name can be displayed in your volunteer biography on the organization's website, for example.

You Are Transitioning from Military to Civilian Life

As a veteran, you bring a unique set of skills and experience gained during your service, including discipline, leadership, teamwork, and adaptability. Yet, when we spoke to some veterans who were transitioning to civilian life, they told us that moving from the organized military world to a regular job can be challenging. One respondent told us, "For veterans, it's hard to figure out and talk about what you've achieved when they try to apply for jobs or get extra certifications like the PMP that requires experience."

We sent a survey to veterans transitioning to the civilian world to gain more insights. The survey revealed that volunteering significantly aids veterans transitioning from military to project management careers. For instance, Brian Kemper shared how volunteering allowed him to give back and learn from others. It helped him recognize the value of his military skills in civilian roles. Brian advises new volunteers to view each opportunity as a project leadership opportunity. He emphasizes the importance of patience and finding a balance during the transition process. Additionally, volunteering exposed Brian to various organizations, highlighting the demand for project management skills across different industries. At the time of the interview, he was involved with the PMI local chapter in outreach activities.

For another respondent, the transition from a career in the US Navy to a local volunteer organization provided valuable insights. In this role, he learned the intricacies of managing agendas and event planning, including catering, based on feedback from attendees. This practical experience enriched his understanding of project management. His advice was focused on engagement and fulfillment: "When volunteering, choose an organization that truly resonates with you, or else you will get bored."

We recommend joining a project management organization that supports veterans. PMI has a specific initiative for veterans, and it extends to the local chapters.

PMI in North America has more than 60 chapters that pay special attention to veterans. The volunteers in this group support bridging the gap between what employers want and how veterans can demonstrate their highly useful skills.

We also had the opportunity to interview Joe Pusz, one of the founders of the Veteran Project Manager Mentor Alliance (VPMMA). VPMMA makes ongoing efforts to enhance its support system, and the organization plays a pivotal role in helping individuals successfully transition to civilian life.

Joe told us that VPMMA, a nonprofit organization, is dedicated to assisting military service members, veterans, and their spouses in transitioning to civilian project management careers. The organization's mission revolves around empowering and equipping individuals with the skills and guidance they need to excel in project management roles. Mentorship is a core aspect of VPMMA's operations, with mentors offering their career insights and contributing to the organization's mission. The VPMMA operates with an entirely volunteer-driven workforce.

While the organization primarily focuses on the USA, it has also had the privilege of collaborating with volunteers from Canada and recently welcomed a Board of Directors member from the United Kingdom.

The heart of VPMMA is project management, and its volunteers come from backgrounds closely related to this field. Joe explained that volunteers vary in terms of their commitment, but on average, they stay for around 2.5 years. What sets VPMMA apart is its virtual operating model, designed for accessibility and online presence from the get-go.

Now that we have looked at these four employment situations, we turn next to leveraging your experiences in your CV and on social media.

DEVELOP YOUR BRAND BY LEVERAGING YOUR CV AND SOCIAL MEDIA

A personal brand allows you to effectively communicate who you are, your expertise, and the value you can bring to others. A personal brand helps you avoid invisibility and allows your uniqueness to shine.[5] You will attract professional opportunities, build credibility and trust, expand your network, and foster personal development.

Volunteering in project roles or organizations will raise your profile, position you as an expert, and increase your visibility as a project leader. Gradually, you will become recognized for your achievements, strong problem-solving, or cultural fluency. People will come to you to ask for advice or mentorship. People may invite you to conferences to share your knowledge or ask you to write for newsletters. People at work will come to you to learn more about your volunteer engagements.

You can boost your personal branding as a project leader by leveraging:

- your CV/resume
- social media

LEVERAGING YOUR CV/RESUME

During our webinars,[6] one particular question resonated with many volunteers: "How can I leverage all this valuable experience in my resume or CV? Is it appropriate to do so, and if yes, how?" Intrigued by this common concern, we sought insights from human resources (HR) experts through a survey.

All the HR experts we interviewed had more than ten years of experience. They worked in Germany, France, India, the USA, and Mexico in different industries: technology, executive recruitment, manufacturing, food and beverages, and automation.

Our HR experts recommend displaying extracurricular activities at the end of your CV.

The Importance of Extracurricular Activities (Including Volunteering) on a CV

Virginie Pires, French business relations consultant in Paris at APEC (French Association for the Employment of Executives), confirmed that these extracurricular activities should be included on your CV.

> It is a mandatory section, but the activities mentioned must show a real commitment beyond a simple interest. Civic engagement, i.e., giving of oneself and contributing to the community, is also part of this section. Having extra-professional activities helps to understand the candidate's personality better.

Role of Volunteer Experiences When You Want to Move to Project Management

For junior positions that don't necessarily require credentials, volunteer experiences can play a positive role in the hiring decision. Credentials, diplomas, and field knowledge are usually necessary for more senior roles, but even in these cases, volunteer experiences can help employers discriminate between candidates.

In situations where there is a shortage of human resources or candidates, employers may have to become more flexible in their hiring criteria and look for other skills.

According to a study carried out by APEC in 2020, employers are looking for candidates who are curious and motivated to acquire new skills.[7] This means being resourceful, finding information, and undertaking training by themselves. Teamwork is also a significant asset, and volunteering contributes to your development as a multifaceted and well-rounded human being.

Virginie Pires confirms that technical skills, experience, and qualifications are still priorities in France, but extra-professional activities can enhance them. As Virginie states, "What is crucial is to formulate and present your activities in line with the position you apply for." Social media can also help you highlight these activities.

LEVERAGING SOCIAL MEDIA

You did it! You volunteered; now is the time to showcase it. We are not suggesting you give yourself an ego boost. However, you should include all your volunteer roles on your professional social media because it will help you find common ground in your network.

Professional social media platforms, such as LinkedIn, have a dedicated section for volunteer roles.

If you decide to display your volunteer roles as part of your work experience section, be transparent about it; write explicitly that this is a volunteer role. For example, you can write, "Social Media Contributor in organization Y (Volunteer)."

CASE STUDY: CAN VOLUNTEERING HELP ME TO PROGRESS IN MY CAREER?

Franca* is a seasoned volunteer. In her day job she is an HR manager. This time, she is volunteering in a team at a local not-for-profit for a year. In this role, she has onboarded new volunteers, designed slides, and created short videos and FAQs. She really strove for smooth integration into the team.

But, one day, they had to create material for an important presentation to find new partners. John*, another volunteer, was responsible for this. In the team meeting, he presented what he had created. Franca gave him good advice on how to improve the presentation. John was so grateful that he asked Franca to be the co-presenter.

The day of the presentation came, and it was a success. A few months later, she was contacted by the head of learning in one of the firms she presented to, who asked her to apply for a paid position as a technical trainer. Would Franca have got the same proposal if she had not volunteered?

Our Views

Volunteering is not a panacea. But if you volunteer strategically, you can make volunteering part of your professional development and career. Franca gained transferable skills: communication, collaboration, and strategic thinking. It helped her to complement her working experiences as an HR manager. She could leverage this new knowledge in her next role. But if you volunteer at a soup kitchen and work in nanotechnology, you can only expect a direct link to your career if your volunteer boss at the soup kitchen is a top manager in a nanotechnology firm. However, volunteering creates serendipitous encounters that can lead to potential jobs.

VOLUNTEERS' STORIES: LUIS ANTONIO GUARDADO RIVERA IN EL SALVADOR

Luis Antonio Guardado Rivera is a multi-award-winning professional and an active volunteer in numerous project management and PMO organizations. His volunteering journey began at the age of 7. At that time, he helped distribute food to vulnerable people. "I think I didn't really understand what I was doing because I was young, but I can confirm that making someone smile with an act of service seemed simply magical to me." Over time, this desire to serve spread to become a fundamental part of all dimensions of his life.

And for him, it translates into education and sharing knowledge to help his country to develop and grow. "Education has been a gift, perhaps one of the greatest, thanks to which I have been entrusted with opportunities that have allowed me to care for my family. Teachers, mentors, and volunteers share their understanding and way of being. They transmit values and inspire you to be better; they facilitate your learning and enhance your skills; they give all of themselves in the classroom and make their work a true vocation of service – certainly, a very noble role in protecting multiple aspects of society, such as culture, academia, and social welfare," Luis told us. He contributes to lectures and is a volunteer board member in several organizations. Volunteering has helped him to stay up to date with the latest trends, to network, to position his personal brand, and ultimately to remain employable. "In my particular case, coming from a small and developing country, it has been a great opportunity to show the world the quality of human capital of El Salvador," he added.

He also pointed out that volunteering nurtures his need for continuous learning.

> I am convinced that, for the professional of the future, stopping learning is a 'non-negotiable'; in my particular case, studying amuses me a lot. Certainly, much of what I study and research is related to the knowledge areas in which I work, but other than that, since I was a teenager, I have been inquisitive and a fan of philosophy. A little over two years ago, I started my Ph.D. in the History of Philosophy. I'm enjoying it a lot. Of course, I am not the most outstanding student in my classes, but imagine how much fun it is for an industrial engineer to speak with anthropologists, sociologists, and philosophers who have been contributing to these areas of study for years.

And what is his own philosophy?

> I believe you cannot be a great professional if you are not a great person first. Honestly, there is no other way. When you volunteer, you do it thinking about putting your gifts at the service of society, but in reality, each of the people you help is the one who ends up helping you, putting a smile on your face and fueling your day-to-day motivation.

Volunteering is a labor of love for him, and he challenges himself daily to become a better project leader and human being. To him, by volunteering, you put your talents at the service of the community, honor life with purpose, and give back to the world the blessings it has given you.

"I truly believe that creating opportunities for others is a way to leave a better world than the one you found," he humbly concluded.

KEY TAKEAWAYS

- By volunteering, you can develop valuable skills for work.
- Volunteering provides benefits if you are unemployed, self-employed, a corporate employee, or transitioning from military to civilian life.
- Leverage your volunteer experiences in your CV and on social media to stand out.

YOUR A.H.A. MOMENT: ACTIVITY, HOPE, ACTION

It's your turn!

ACTIVITY

Answer the questions below:

- How can volunteering help you remain employable?
- How can you leverage your volunteering activities in your CV?
- What can you leverage in social media about your volunteering activities that will benefit your project leader brand?

HOPE

What is your main hope regarding your employability by volunteering?
Prompt: "By volunteering, I hope to remain employable in these aspects: ..."

ACTION

Write down an action you want to take in the next three months to remain employable.

NOTES

1 Kanter, R. M. (1995). Nice Work if You Can Get It: The Software Industry as a Model for Tomorrow's Jobs. *American Prospect*, (23), 52–58.
2 Lyons, M. (2023, March 17). Keeping Your Confidence Up during a Lengthy Job Search. *Harvard Business Review*. https://hbr.org/2023/03/keeping-your-confidence-up-during-a-lengthy-job-search
3 Clark, D. (2021). *The Long Game: How to Be a Long-Term Thinker in a Short-Term World*. Harvard Business Review Press.
4 Leap to Success. (n.d.). About. https://leaptosuccessatx.org/about/
5 Michail, J. (2020, April). How Does Personal Brand Leadership Work and Why Is It Critical? *Forbes*. https://www.forbes.com/sites/forbescoachescouncil/2020/04/17/how-does-personal-brand-leadership-work-and-why-is-it-critical/
6 Khelifi, Y., & Mata Sivera, M., 4 Ways Volunteering Will Make You a Better Project Manager for the New Normal (available with a PMI Membership) on projectmanagement.com, December 17, 2021; Khelifi, Y., & Mata Sivera, M., 4 formas en que el voluntariado le convertirá en un mejor gerente de proyectos para la nueva normalidad, in Spanish (available with a PMI Membership) on projectmanagement.com, November 11, 2022.
7 APEC. (n.d.). L'identification des compétences dans le recrutement de cadres. APEC. https://corporate.apec.fr/home/nos-etudes/toutes-nos-etudes/lidentification-des-competences.html

Part III

Plan Your Career Development by Volunteering

8 How to Identify Volunteering Goals That Align with Your Career Goals

The only way to think like a leader is first to plunge yourself into new projects and activities, interact with very different kinds of people, and experiment with unfamiliar ways of getting things done.[1]

Herminia Ibarra
Author of Act Like a Leader, Think Like a Leader

This chapter will focus on goals, SMART (Specific, Measurable, Achievable, Relevant, Time-bound) goals, and how to match your activities with your SMART goals. While you may well enjoy volunteering as a worthwhile activity in itself, you can also set goals for your volunteer activities that align with your career aspirations. This strategic approach to volunteering will maximize the impact of your volunteer experiences, making all your activities and tasks valuable for your professional growth as a project leader.

WHY IS IT ESSENTIAL TO THINK ABOUT YOUR VOLUNTEERING GOALS?

When you enter the volunteering world, you will face several choices regarding opportunities, activities, and roles. If you think ahead about what you'd like to get from your role, you will maximize your effectiveness and personal fulfillment. You will remain purposefully engaged: you won't just show up because you need to but because it matters to you, and you are serving a cause. You can prioritize what will help you reach your goals, enhancing your sense of impact and accomplishment. You will remain motivated along the journey: a sense of purpose and direction fuels enthusiasm and persistence, keeping you engaged and committed to making a difference. But how do you identify your goals?

IDENTIFY YOUR HIGH-LEVEL GOALS

A goal is a broad statement that expresses your desired outcomes in the longer term. To identify your goals, you must clarify your values, passion, and purpose.

DOI: 10.1201/9781003407942-11

CLARIFY YOUR VALUES, PASSION, AND PURPOSE FOR VOLUNTEERING

In a *Harvard Business Review* article, Irina Cozma, executive coach, provides a framework for thinking about your values, passion, and purpose, which can help you identify your goals before embarking on your volunteering journey.[2]

Your Values

The values are your foundation, what is important to you, and what you cannot negotiate on. Clarifying your values will help you select an organization to volunteer for (we will discuss this in Chapter 9).

📋 Write down your values in the Goals section of My Volunteering Canvas.

Your Passion

Your passion gives you energy and emotion. It is what you enjoy doing. You don't need an external reward to make you do it. You are intrinsically motivated. You can have several passions, and they can evolve with time.

📋 Write down your passion in the Goals section of My Volunteering Canvas.

Your Purpose

Your purpose is the essence of your existence. It gives a concrete direction to your engagement to achieve goals.

📋 Write down your purpose in the Goals section of My Volunteering Canvas.

TWO REAL-LIFE EXAMPLES

Mark Cawood, an IPMA South African member, told us:

> In South Africa, we have many challenges, such as economic inequality, unemployment, and broad access to quality education and health, to name a few. There are, therefore, many opportunities to make a difference, and this has motivated me and many others to volunteer our time towards building a better future for the nation that we love.

That is also the purpose of Danny Byabene, a former board member volunteer at the PMI Democratic Republic of Congo chapter. He'd like to set up a platform where volunteers can be called for consultation and recommendation.

> Professional organizations can also help shape the education system to prepare future professionals considering the industry's standard and state-of-the-art techniques and principles. Volunteers and members of these professional organizations will come from the private sector, the country's international organizations, and even the diaspora.

To him, volunteers will impact the community and the country while developing their skills. They will shape the professions and the practice in their field.

The desire to shape a better future for your country can be a profound motivation, as it is for Mark and Danny. High-level goals like these will be your beacon and guide you in your volunteering journey.

Once you have identified your goals, you must define more concrete objectives to accomplish them – and this is where SMART goals can help.

IDENTIFY YOUR SMART GOALS

A SMART goal is a specific target you want to achieve to support your high-level goals.

We will start with a real case to help you understand how to identify them.

Darkhantsetseg Erdenetsogt (Dana), a volunteer board member in the PMI Mongolia chapter, aligned her personal goals with her volunteer roles. To her, identifying personal goals in the volunteering setting involves understanding what you want to achieve in your professional growth and how you can make a meaningful contribution to your community.

> When I decided to volunteer, I tried to align my personal goals with the organization's mission and contribute in a way that mattered. I took the time to reflect on my professional aspirations and areas where I wanted to grow. One of my goals was to expand my professional network and connect with fellow project management professionals. I recognized the value of learning from their experiences, gaining insights into different industries, and building relationships that could benefit my career. With this in mind, I actively sought volunteer roles involving collaboration and networking, such as joining event planning committees or assisting with the finance teams.
>
> Another goal I had was to enhance my leadership skills. As an investment analyst, I understood the importance of developing the ability to lead teams, influence stakeholders, and drive successful outcomes. To achieve this, I looked for volunteer opportunities that allowed me to take on leadership responsibilities, such as serving on the board or assuming positions of responsibility within the organization's structure.
>
> Additionally, I aimed to contribute my knowledge and expertise to the project management community in Mongolia. Giving back to the community and the country that had provided me with so much was deeply important. To fulfill this goal, I actively participated in organizing events, promoted their activities within my circle of influence, and provided support within their financial team for the past five years.

So, Dana had two goals: professional development through networking and leadership skills, and supporting her country's project management community by sharing her own knowledge about project management.

Her two goals are not contradictory: she can develop professionally while she also helps the project management community. Then, she looked for activities to support her goals. Such clarity of purpose is highly beneficial.

From now on, we will define SMART goals for your career development through three lenses:

- the leadership skills you want to acquire
- the network you want to expand
- the new fields you want to explore

Write down your SMART goals for skills, networking, and new fields in the Goals section of My Volunteering Canvas.

SMART GOALS FOR LEADERSHIP SKILLS

Look back at the six leadership skills we described at the start of Chapter 3. What is your level of mastery of each skill on a scale of 0–5 (where 0 is the lowest)? This assessment will allow you to see the areas where you need to develop most. It is useful to formulate your goal first in a general way (which we call a "foggy goal"), and then make it SMART.

Example:

Foggy goal: I want to improve my communication in a global environment.

SMART goal: This year, I will take part in two activities in an international team and make one presentation in English in front of an audience.

SMART GOALS FOR NETWORK GROWTH

Look back at your self-assessment of your networking skills in Table 5.1. Again, you can see the areas where you need to develop most and formulate your goals.

Example:

Foggy goal: I want to improve my networking skills.

SMART goal: I want to maintain contact with two new peers for six months. I want to talk twice with them in person to get to know them better. I need to remember what interests them and send them relevant information.

SMART GOALS FOR EXPLORING NEW FIELDS

Identify a skill you'd like to practice or an activity you'd like to experiment with and formulate your goals.

Example:

Foggy goal: I want to experiment with new things, like displaying visual information better in presentations.

SMART goal: This year, I will volunteer to create impactful visuals for the team's presentations. I will ask for feedback from communication experts in the organization, and I will refine them. I will compare the first visuals I created and the revised ones to understand what I improved.

In Chapter 10, you will find out how you can match your goals to your volunteering activities.

CASE STUDY: WHY AM I VOLUNTEERING?

Pape* is a young project manager in construction. Like his alumni friends, he has volunteered in a project management organization since university. At work, there is a volunteer project management group, and they are looking for someone to develop the program of events for the year. Pape volunteered to do it because it was an opportunity to gain visibility. He was accepted. But now, after a few months, he is not motivated anymore. He doesn't know why he is there. He has just been offered a different opportunity to present a webinar about project management in construction. Should Pape accept?

OUR VIEWS

Pape should not accept right away. He must take time to understand his goals and SMART objectives. Does he want to learn a new skill? Does he want to expand his network? Does he like to explore new fields? When he has reflected on this, he can make a sound decision.

VOLUNTEERS' STORIES: LEE R. LAMBERT IN THE USA

Lee R. Lambert is one of the founders of the Project Management Professional (PMP), the internationally renowned PMI project certification. Lee never tires of jumping on a plane to spread the word about project management and the PMI organization. He looks forward to each opportunity to meet new people and discover new cultures. Lee has met many PMI volunteers and is one of the best advocates for volunteering. He has been volunteering for more than 50 years.

"I began volunteering in 1968 when I joined the Jaycees, a young men's civic organization for community service,"[3] he told us.

> I fell in love with young men sacrificing their time to accomplish great things through volunteering. It all started when my wife said I should find something to occupy my spare time. She suggested the Jaycees, and I have been volunteering ever since. I eventually became the President of the Year in California in 1975.

Since 1968, he has volunteered in various organizations, including Jaycees, youth baseball programs, and PMI. He led, organized, and recruited additional volunteers in most roles. Many of the volunteer projects he was in charge of won national recognition as the project of the year in a variety of categories.

Throughout his career, one thing has been clear:

> My family's needs monitor my work–life balance. If they need me, I am there … I have learned to judge if I am out of balance. It is critical that I also pay attention to other volunteers who get out of balance.

Looking back, there is one thing he wishes he had known: the power of the saying, "What's in it for me, what's in it for you, and what's in it for the organization." According to Lee, volunteers do things for *their* reasons – not yours. There must be something in it for the volunteer, even if it is a sense of self-satisfaction.

Volunteering is an opportunity to make a difference; by doing so, people can feel a greater sense of accomplishment and contribution. He constantly gauges his feelings to confirm if he is in his comfort zone or not. If he is firmly in his comfort zone, he is not expanding his horizons. "The more I feel out of my comfort zone, the more I learn new things. Get out of your comfort zone and grow your capabilities and career."

KEY TAKEAWAYS

- Clarifying your values, passion, and purpose will help you to identify your volunteering goals.

- You can have goals for your organization, country, and yourself that are not contradictory.
- SMART goals are your beacon during your volunteering journey to grow as a project leader.

YOUR A.H.A. MOMENT: ACTIVITY, HOPE, ACTION

It's your turn!

ACTIVITY

Answer the questions below:

- What are your high-level goals for volunteering?
- What skills would you like to improve?
- What are your two main SMART goals?

HOPE

What do you hope to achieve by volunteering?
Prompt: "By volunteering, I hope to achieve a SMART goal related to…"

ACTION

Write down one action you want to take in the next three months to achieve your two main SMART goals.

NOTES

1 Ibarra, H. (2015). *Act Like a Leader, Think Like a Leader*. Harvard Business Review Press.
2 Cozma, I. (2023, October 23). Values, Passion, or Purpose — Which Should Guide Your Career? *Harvard Business Review*. https://hbr.org/2023/10/values-passion-or-purpose-which-should-guide-your-career
3 The United States Junior Chamber, also known as the Jaycees, JCs, or JCI USA, is a leadership training service and civic organization for people aged between 18 and 40. It is a branch of Junior Chamber International (JCI).

9 How to Find the Right Organization to Complement Your Professional Aspirations

Volunteering is the ability to give part of yourself to people without expecting anything in return. My thirty years of volunteering experience allowed me to grow, and to provide a certain sense of fulfillment for the people I served and to myself. I hope to continue to share this gift through volunteering for the good of society.

Amin Saidoun
Executive Director of IPMA

This chapter will guide you in finding the proper projectized organization outside or within your firm that complements your professional development. For that, you need to resonate with the organization's mission and values and find an opportunity that fits your busy timetable: volunteer roles can be in person, virtual, and hybrid, with pros and cons we will explore to help you decide.

ASSESS THE MISSION AND VALUES OF THE ORGANIZATION

If an organization's mission and values align with your own interests and motivations, you are more likely to be committed and engaged. Take the time to explore the website of each organization you are interested in. Review its mission, values, and culture.

During early conversations with other volunteers or representatives of the organization, you can ask a few questions that will help you discover if the organization's mission and values fit with your own:

- What are the organization's mission and values? And how do they guide the work of volunteers?
- Could you share an example of a volunteer project aligned with the organization's mission and values?
- Are there resources to ensure that volunteers understand and uphold the mission and values of the organization?

Preparing questions like these demonstrates your willingness to engage in the volunteer role, especially if you are being interviewed for the role; while it might seem unusual to have a job interview for a volunteer position, it does occasionally occur.

DOI: 10.1201/9781003407942-12

Freddy Andale, a project manager in the banking sector in Papua New Guinea, scrutinized organizations' missions before volunteering. "First, I wanted to support an organization improving its governance structure and ensuring accountability and transparency; second, I wanted to participate in initiatives that directly benefited marginalized groups and addressed their needs and challenges." He volunteers for two organizations: Australia Pacific Youth Dialogue and Save the Children Papua New Guinea. They both aim to empower young people and promote their rights and well-being in the region.

Before giving you the tools to search for an appropriate organization, let's review the different forms of volunteering and how you can choose the right one: in person, virtual, or hybrid.

VOLUNTEERING CAN BE IN PERSON, VIRTUAL, OR HYBRID

Years ago, volunteering typically involved physically going to a location and was limited to local activities. In 1996, the Virtual Volunteering Project was launched, thanks to Steve Glikbarg and Cindy Shove, co-founders of Impact Online (which became Volunteer Match).[1] Since then, with the development of working from home and global teams, virtual volunteering has become a practical and effective way to make a difference.

With just a computer and an internet connection, you can now connect with organizations worldwide and contribute to projects. Lately, hybrid collaboration has increased, in response to people's needs for human contact and flexibility.

So, volunteering can take three forms, and they can be combined:

* in person
* virtual
* hybrid

Here are the benefits of each of them.

In Person

This is the more conventional way to volunteer. You get to know people in your local communities. In this case, check your commuting time. If you need public transportation, ensure you have efficient options. If you will be driving, check the route beforehand.

Eliott* is a remote project leader for a large software firm. He has realized he needs more human interaction and wants to see people beyond his computer screen. Additionally, after more than five years of working remotely, he has noticed that he has lost his presence in meetings. He tends to turn off the camera and roll his eyes when he disagrees with something, rather than expressing his views.

Eliott has started looking for in-person volunteer opportunities to enhance his presence during meetings and avoid disengaging while under stress or when he doesn't align with the views of the leadership. These opportunities will allow him to engage and improve his interpersonal skills more meaningfully and actively.

VIRTUAL

In virtual opportunities, you can collaborate with colleagues from literally all corners of the world. Being a virtual volunteer doesn't mean you don't want to meet people or collaborate. You can choose to volunteer online for various reasons.[2] There may be no in-person volunteer opportunities in your neighborhood. You may want to volunteer online for an organization for which you already volunteer on-site because there are new opportunities in another region. Maybe you have some disabilities that prevent you from traveling. Or maybe you are looking for flexible volunteer hours or want to save commuting time. Or perhaps you have never collaborated in a virtual-only environment and want to challenge yourself.

These days, even board roles can be conducted through virtual volunteering. For example, Arief Prasetyo, senior integration project manager in an energy company in Saudi Arabia, is a remote board member volunteer at the PMI Indonesia chapter. He insists on one point: "Take every opportunity possible to attend physical gatherings, even once a year, once a quarter. Don't forget to build real connections and befriend fellow volunteers." As he rightly says, being a remote volunteer can make you feel disconnected from the team. "If you are in a different time zone, you may also feel that you are missing out on discussions and do not have the sense of urgency."

In the world of virtual volunteering, you will also have to become proficient with different online tools, but you must ask if there are technical requirements (software, webcam, sound) and find out if the webcam must always be on (which can impact your bandwidth).

HYBRID

The advantage of hybrid volunteer opportunities is that you can still contribute to activities even in your own country with more flexibility from the comfort of your home. And at the same time, you can get together and meet people face-to-face if you wish. When you opt for a hybrid volunteer role, you must check how often there are face-to-face meetings, and if those are local or if you need to travel to another location. If you need to attend meetings that are a long way from home, remember to check with the organization whether the cost of travel and accommodation is reimbursed.

What's the best solution? Should you volunteer for a virtual opportunity or in person? It depends on your personal and psychological preferences and what you are trying to achieve professionally. If you love meeting people face-to-face, an organization that offers in-person or hybrid activities and roles will suit you better. If you have a hectic life but want to give back, a short virtual-only option is best. Some organizations favor in-person volunteering, and others do not. Pay attention to this criterion (which should be indicated in the advertisement for the post) when you are looking for a projectized organization.

▯ Fill in the Criteria section of My Volunteering Canvas.

HOW TO FIND AN OPPORTUNITY IN PROJECTIZED ORGANIZATIONS

When looking for an appropriate projectized organization, nonprofit organizations, nongovernmental organizations (NGOs), and grassroots organizations could be good first candidates. You can search for an organization through:

- dedicated platforms
- websites
- word of mouth
- organizations' events
- your own workplace

In Part II, we have also mentioned specific organizations for the unemployed or veterans.

DEDICATED PLATFORMS

Some popular platforms include VolunteerMatch (www.volunteermatch.org), Idealist (www.idealist.org), and All for Good (www.allforgood.org). These platforms allow you to search for volunteer opportunities based on location, cause, or specific skills. There are also local platforms, such as https://volunteers.ae/ in the United Arab Emirates.

WEBSITES

Explore the websites of the organizations you want to collaborate with. Additionally, you can subscribe to their newsletters and communications on their websites to get regular updates.

WORD OF MOUTH

The power of personal recommendation is priceless. If a good friend volunteers in an organization you are interested in, they can inform you of new opportunities. Inform your network you are looking for a new volunteer role, and be clear about your career goals and what you want to learn in the new role.

ORGANIZATIONS' EVENTS

There might be a forthcoming conference or annual event for the organization you are interested in. And volunteers may be needed. This is a way to get a foot in the door. You might hear that someone is leaving a role or that support is needed to revive a community of practice. This is also a way to forge new relationships and inform the organization you are keen on helping with future projects.

YOUR OWN WORKPLACE

Some companies have volunteer programs or initiatives that give employees opportunities to give back to the community – and to learn skills. An exploratory study of 278 respondents to an online survey in the USA found that employees saw corporate volunteering as an effective way of developing job-related skills, especially teamwork.[3]

Also, in the USA, some organizations offer paid volunteer hours, which means you receive compensation for your work while contributing to nonprofit organizations.[4]

Some organizations also have Employee Resource Groups (ERGs). ERGs are usually voluntary, employee-led groups. Ask your manager or human resources department if such groups exist in your organization.

Arief Prasetyo, whom we met earlier in this chapter, also volunteers in his workplace to share his knowledge and connect with colleagues.

> I am the community leader for a group of people passionate about project management. I have served for two consecutive periods now. Besides the usual webinars and workshops to expand people's knowledge, this community is also a support system for project professionals within the company to progress with their careers. There are over 4,000 members of this community, from different functions of the organizations and spread all over the world.

WHAT IF YOU CAN'T FIND A SUITABLE ROLE?

Don't be discouraged if you can't find a suitable role in an organization or within your workplace! Organizations don't advertise all their positions on their website. Hence, looking for roles in different ways and keeping an ear to the ground for opportunities is essential. Remember, there are hidden opportunities.

Meanwhile, you can create your own learning paths! You can set up a lunch and discuss initiatives with your peers. Or you can check if communities of practice or communities of experts exist or if you can build one.

CASE STUDY: WHAT SHOULD I DO WHEN THERE IS NO ROLE AVAILABLE?

Liu* is a newly certified project manager who has been searching without success for a volunteer role in projectized organizations. His goal was to engage with the community and improve his networking skills. He applied to three different organizations. One organization mentioned that they currently don't have any available positions, while another required someone with a different background. The third organization did not respond at all.

In a conversation with Lana*, a colleague at work, Liu learned that Lana has been volunteering in a workplace community focused on Agile for a few weeks. The community has an open position in the outreach team, aiming to establish more partnerships with universities. Liu is unsure about this opportunity because he primarily wants to volunteer in a projectized organization. However, he is uncertain when a new volunteer opportunity will become available in his preferred projectized organization.

Should Liu take on this volunteer role in his workplace?

Our Views

Yes, Liu should take on this role. Volunteering in project management doesn't stop at projectized organizations. Liu may find that his work on the outreach team is full of networking opportunities inside and outside his organization.

VOLUNTEERS' STORIES: FATIMAH ABBOUCHI IN AUSTRALIA

Fatimah Abbouchi, chief executive officer of an Australian boutique consulting firm, embarked on her journey of giving back at a young age. Fueled by curiosity and a desire to try new things, she embraced opportunities to contribute to her community.

Reflecting on her motivation for volunteering, Fatimah explains, "I was a social child who enjoyed trying new things and seizing every opportunity. Volunteering allowed me to explore and learn without the burden of risks companies often face when providing opportunities to gain relevant experience."

From working in the school canteen to organizing events and even dedicating her time at a local nursing home, Fatimah's early volunteering experiences supported her appreciation for personal development and the power of helping others.

We chatted with Fatimah about how to find volunteer roles. She mentioned that finding volunteer roles can be more accessible with the help of various platforms like LinkedIn jobs, national volunteering websites, and job boards. She explained that by keeping an eye out for these opportunities, you can discover available volunteer positions almost everywhere.

When asked about her advice for fellow volunteers, Fatimah emphasizes the importance of following one's passion. She says:

> Volunteering is all about giving your time and resources to support a cause you care deeply about. When you align your volunteer work with your passions, you make a meaningful impact and find personal fulfillment and growth in the process.

You can also leverage social media by simply expressing your interest in volunteering. Another approach is to contact specific organizations you wish to work with and inquire about potential volunteer opportunities. They can provide a valuable chance to showcase your skills and open doors for future endeavors.

Fatimah's journey exemplifies the impact volunteering can have on one's career. Her first job was a direct result of her volunteer experience, which opened doors to a three-and-a-half-year retail position, enabling her to progress from a customer service attendant to a store supervisor.

Balancing work and volunteering is a challenge that Fatimah approaches with careful consideration. Fatimah ensures she can contribute effectively while running her business smoothly by selecting a few organizations to volunteer with at a time and aligning her volunteering efforts with the ebb and flow of her work commitments.

In terms of what triggers her to stop volunteering, Fatimah shares her experience of discontinuing her involvement with an organization that displayed unkindness, injustice, unfairness, or unreasonable behavior towards volunteers. "Organizations need to respect and appreciate their volunteers and remember they are doing this to give back, which should be appreciated," she told us.

Sharing her perspective on the role of volunteering in personal and professional development, Fatimah says:

> Volunteering has been an incredible opportunity to step outside my comfort zone, meet new people, and gain a deeper understanding of diverse experiences. It has shaped my career by providing me with insights into different industries and teaching me valuable skills that I would have never had the opportunity to acquire.

What is essential is to follow your passion. "By volunteering, you can pick up skills and experiences that you would otherwise never have had the opportunity to do. When we volunteer, we spread love. We spread the care."

KEY TAKEAWAYS

- Assessing organizations' values and missions will help you select a list of organizations you want to volunteer for – and at the same time, that complement your career expertise or interests.
- You can volunteer in person, virtually, or in a hybrid way.
- You can look for roles in projectized organizations or within your workplace.

YOUR A.H.A. MOMENT: ACTIVITY, HOPE, ACTION

It's your turn!

ACTIVITY

Answer the questions below:

- What values are essential for you in an organization?
- How can you look for appropriate organizations?
- What volunteer communities are there in your workplace?

HOPE

What kind of organizations do you hope to join as a volunteer?
Prompt: "I'd like to join an organization that ..."

ACTION

Write down an action you want to take within the next three months to explore a new volunteer organization, or evaluate whether your current organization's mission and values are still aligned with your professional aspirations.

NOTES

1 Cravens, J. (2016, December). 20 Years Ago: The Virtual Volunteering Project. Jayne Cravens Blog. http://coyotecommunications.com/coyoteblog/2016/12/vvproject20/
2 Cravens, J., & Ellis, S. (2014). *The Last Virtual Volunteering Guidebook: Fully Integrating Online Service into Volunteer Involvement.* Energize, Inc.
3 Peterson, D. K. (2004). Benefits of Participation in Corporate Volunteer Programs: Employees' Perceptions. *Personnel Review*, 33(6), 615–627. https://doi.org/10.1108/00483480410561510
4 LaPonsie, M. (2022, June 16). What Is Paid Time off to Volunteer? *US News Money.* https://money.usnews.com/careers/articles/what-is-paid-time-off-to-volunteer

10 How to Choose Activities That Enhance Your Career in Project Leadership

Volunteering is a crucial aspect of one's professional life. Early in your career, volunteering can dramatically increase one's learning process. Later, it becomes a way to give back to one's profession; volunteering becomes a professional obligation. Volunteering is also about helping others, which can profoundly impact one's personal development, self-confidence, and career. These benefits were and continue to be apparent and robust in my career.

David L. Pells
PMI Fellow, HonFAPM, Editor of PM World Journal

This chapter will help you identify suitable volunteering activities to achieve your career goals.

IDENTIFY SUITABLE ACTIVITIES

There are different categories of volunteer activities in projectized organizations. The organization's website can give you insights into the various domains and their activities.

Some examples are listed below. However, bear in mind that this list is not exhaustive. It is just intended to show you some of the broad and diverse opportunities you can find to support your career growth.

MARKETING AND COMMUNICATION

You can write articles or create a newsletter. You can also create marketing materials, leaflets, videos, podcasts, and visuals.

SOCIAL MEDIA

You can create posts, visuals, or marketing campaigns to advertise the events and accomplishments of your community.

EVENTS

You can organize webinars or face-to-face events. You can choose the speakers and liaise with them. You can also be a speaker yourself or moderate a discussion panel.

DOI: 10.1201/9781003407942-13

The organization may hold a major annual event. You can lead this project or be part of the team that arranges it.

COMMUNITIES OF PRACTICE OR SPECIAL INTEREST GROUPS

Communities of Practice (CoPs) and Special Interest Groups (SIGs) consist of professionals working in the same field, sector, or industry. They meet to share best practices, support each other's development, advance a topic, and influence the industry. You can contribute to one of these, or even lead one.

PARTNERSHIPS AND OUTREACH TEAMS

You can develop external relationships with universities or enterprises and, for example, organize joint events.

FINANCE

You can manage the budget of a project or of the organization at the board level.

GOVERNANCE

You can manage legal and regulatory aspects. You can ensure that rules follow the local legislation. You can help to define roles in the organization.

VOLUNTEER TEAM

You can develop content for volunteers, mentor the new ones, or facilitate knowledge transfer. You can also be the volunteer liaison. Or you can organize volunteer meet-ups to help them network. You can devise a strategy for volunteer recognition: awards, prizes, and ways of sharing volunteers' success stories.

MEMBERSHIP TEAM

Data analysts are needed for member database management. You can organize surveys for members and highlight improvements to make.

WEBSITE ADMINISTRATION

You can help maintain and/or update the website. You can also help to change the website provider or redesign the website's structure.

DIVERSITY AND INCLUSION

This cross-functional domain supports different groups, from outreach to membership and events. Most organizations have specific roles in this area to support minorities inside the organizations.

You already identified your volunteering goals and SMART (Specific, Measurable, Achievable, Realistic, and Time-bound) goals in Chapter 8. Now, let us look at how you can match these to relevant activities. And you can also review the SMART goals you defined earlier.

⊟ Fill out the Activities section in My Volunteering Canvas.

ACTIVITIES TO HONE YOUR SKILLS

As you can see in Figure 10.1, matching activities to your SMART goals is an iterative learning process. In Chapter 8, you identified your SMART goals for each skill. Here, you will select the activity that matches your SMART goal. You'll practice and then apply it to work.

Table 10.1 consolidates the skills we looked at in Chapters 3 and 4 with examples of goals, SMART goals, and possible activities, to show you how to develop your strategy.

FOUR CRITERIA FOR CHOOSING ACTIVITIES STRATEGICALLY

When choosing activities, you should pay attention to the skills required, but also to other factors, like the number of meetings, and the type of communication involved. It will help you select activities that spark joy and allow you to grow as a project

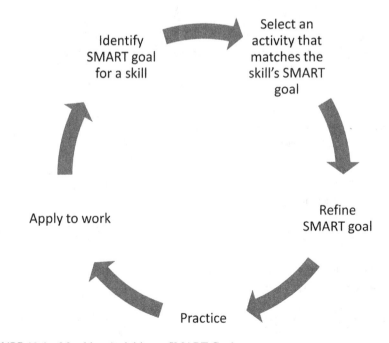

FIGURE 10.1 Matching Activities to SMART Goals

TABLE 10.1

Some Examples of Skills, SMART Goals, and Activities

Skill	Goal	SMART Goal	Activities
Tailor leadership style	I want to practice various leadership styles.	I want to identify and master one distinct leadership style and apply it.	Find a volunteer role where you can practice a style that is not your preferred one.
Communication	I want to improve my English business writing.	I want to write three blogs a year.	Write blogs or articles for the communication team.
Collaboration	I want to collaborate more virtually.	I want to improve my virtual collaboration skills by participating in at least two virtual team projects.	Find a team with remote team members.
Motivating teams	I want to learn to motivate a team.	I want to learn about three motivational theories. I want to lead a project where I can practice the motivational theories.	Lead a project with at least two people.
Problem-solving	I want to enhance my problem-solving skills.	I want to enhance my problem-solving skills by mastering a problem-solving framework.	Participate in one interdisciplinary project within the organization or community.
Strategic thinking	I want to develop a long-term vision.	I want to build my career long-term vision by the end of the year.	Develop a project timeline to visualize the activities and milestones required to achieve the long-term career vision.
Exploring new fields	I want to learn about marketing.	I want to learn about marketing by collaborating on one marketing project.	Complete at least two online courses in marketing fundamentals. Engage in a volunteer opportunity within the marketing team.
Remaining curious	I want to learn more about finance.	I will participate in one finance course in the coming year and talk with the finance team.	"Interview" the finance team.
Networking	I want to get to know more peers in my field.	I want to get to know six new people in six months.	Contribute to a community of practice.

leader. Remember that volunteering is a two-way commitment. Let us review four criteria for choosing activities strategically:

- the type of activity
- the time commitment

- communication methods
- recognition of your efforts

For each criterion, we share some questions you can ask during the interview for a volunteer role or during conversations with other volunteers.

Fill in the Criteria section of My Volunteering Canvas if relevant.

Type of Activity

To manage your expectations correctly, you must understand the characteristics of the activity. From the outset, you can enquire:

- Is it a time-limited activity or an ongoing one?
- Is it in person, virtual, or hybrid?
- How long am I expected to engage in the activity, and what is the process for stopping?

Time Commitment

First, you must have a good idea of how much time is required for the activity. We have already discussed time management in Chapter 4, where we explained that you need to be realistic with your time commitment.

The second piece of advice is to start slow and small with a limited schedule. You'll have the chance to get a taste of what it's like to volunteer at the organization and whether it works for you. Then, you can evaluate whether you'd like to take on more responsibility. Don't overcommit: be sure to deliver what you promised, as we discussed in Chapter 4's section "Managing Your Commitment Level."

Here are some questions you can ask:

- How many hours per week on average does the activity take?
- If the activity involves meetings, do they take place at the weekend or in the evening?
- What if I cannot commit?

Communication Methods

Each organization has a unique way of communicating, and understanding the tools and methods used will help you excel in your new role. You can ask a few questions before joining a new volunteer team:

- How does the team communicate: email or instant messaging?
- How is information and knowledge shared?
- What does the meeting schedule and frequency look like?

RECOGNITION OF YOUR EFFORTS

Do you crave recognition or prefer to work behind the scenes? Whatever your preference, it is important to find out how the organization recognizes the work of its volunteers. Some form of recognition is essential, as it shows that the organization cares about volunteers and acknowledges their efforts. You don't volunteer just to get credit, but expressions of gratitude increase volunteers' sense of belonging and create a good atmosphere.

Cultural values can influence the type of recognition that is given. At a conference, Mayte found herself in a conversation about volunteer recognition. One of the members of an American organization explained that most of their volunteers are government workers. Due to certain restrictions, they couldn't tag individuals in photos on social media platforms and thereby recognize their volunteer time. Instead, they send an individual email to each volunteer, with a certificate, including an acknowledgment of the hours they have dedicated to volunteering.

As conversations continued, another attendee at the conference mentioned that some members, for religious reasons, didn't particularly appreciate receiving birthday greetings. Mayte has been able to apply what she has learned in her day job. When she wants to acknowledge a stakeholder or celebrate their birthday, she asks them in advance. It has enhanced her rapport with her peers and demonstrates her leadership growth.

These anecdotes highlight the significance of recognition, how it can be influenced by culture, and why you should be curious about it.

Here are some questions to think about:

- How do you want your volunteering efforts to be recognized or celebrated?
- What forms of volunteer recognition does the organization offer (e.g., certificate, awards)?
- Can volunteers get a reference letter if needed?

CASE STUDY: SHOULD I TAKE ON ANOTHER VOLUNTEER ACTIVITY?

Kofi* is an IT specialist working in a telecom company. As a volunteer, he writes articles, blogs, and newsletters for a local nonprofit. He is a gifted writer and loves it. One day, a former childhood friend, Abebi*, called him and said, "I need someone to write regularly for my newsletter." Abebi manages a marketing agency. "I've read your articles on the website and loved them," she added. Kofi could not resist the praise. "No problem," he replied, "I'd be glad to help you." A few days later, another friend asked Kofi to speak for free at a forthcoming conference. Kofi was curious to take on this challenge. So, again, he accepted. His "boss" at the nonprofit was organizing a networking event and asked Kofi to come to interview some people. "We will have good material for the next newsletter," he told him.

Then, suddenly, a technical issue arose at Kofi's day job and needed his full attention. He realized he would be unable to manage his volunteer activities and wondered why he had accepted so many.

How should Kofi prioritize these different requests?

OUR VIEWS

Curiosity is good, but it can be overwhelming when it becomes the fear of missing out. Kofi should ask himself these questions:

- What are the timelines and time commitments for each volunteering activity?
- What will he learn in this volunteer opportunity? For example, he has written blogs and articles. What about writing case studies? Kofi could expand his writing skills.
- What visibility will he gain?
- What level of mastery does he want to reach?
- What does he enjoy doing?

VOLUNTEERS' STORIES: BADR BURSHAID IN THE KINGDOM OF SAUDI ARABIA

Badr Burshaid began his volunteering journey by chance when asked if he was interested in joining the project management community in Saudi Arabia. The request was made to improve the profession and align it with the development needs outlined in Saudi Arabia's Vision 2030, a unique transformative economic and social reform blueprint launched by the Saudi Arabian government. Badr was motivated to volunteer his time and skills to contribute to the stewardship of knowledge management for project management, as well as to improve certification processes and promote collaboration among all professionals in Saudi Arabia. He also wanted to create a community to help societies and individuals enhance their capabilities to deliver more efficiently.

Badr is conscious of the importance of his board role as president of the PMI Kingdom of Saudi Arabia chapter (PMI KSA). "I am deeply passionate about using my position as an incubator for knowledge within the community. I am committed to creating an environment that fosters learning, growth, and collaboration and helps connect individuals and organizations across sectors."

He explains that one of his key responsibilities is to serve as a bridge between government and private firms, knowledge and university institutes, nonprofit organizations, and technology providers by facilitating connections and partnerships between these groups. He believes that together they can achieve a more significant impact and drive positive change in the project management industry in Saudi Arabia. And he has already proved this by creating a global project management forum that gathers together the most influential speakers in the world. "This has been an eye-opening experience that has broadened my perspective and given me new insights into the global challenges and opportunities facing project management professionals."

He is also dedicated to increasing the certification level of all professionals in the field and providing them with the necessary support and resources to achieve such certifications. He firmly believes that by investing in the development of PMI KSA chapter members and the wider community, project management standards can be elevated and progress can be driven in Saudi Arabia.

Badr likes helping people to grow. He doesn't track the time he invests in volunteering. For him, volunteering is not just a hobby or something he does on the side – it's a way of life! He is incredibly passionate about giving back to the community and making a positive impact. He considers volunteering to be just as critical as any job.

It is a great realization to understand how fulfilling it can be to give back to humanity through volunteering. The opportunity to contribute to the world and make a positive impact is enriching and provides a sense of self-satisfaction that is hard to match through other means.

Volunteering is an incredible way to become a better leader, and his advice for volunteers is to focus on developing consistency, excellence, and determination. Volunteers can build a track record of success that can translate into other areas of their lives, including the workplace. This dedication and determination can inspire others to follow their lead and help them become more effective and influential leaders.

We asked Badr three specific questions. Here are his answers.

a. *What are the essential criteria to consider for a volunteer role?*
  1. **Passion and interest**. The most crucial factor when choosing a volunteer role is finding something you are passionate about and interested in. It will ensure that you are motivated to give your time and energy to the cause and will be more likely to make a meaningful impact.
  2. **Time commitment**. It's essential to consider how much time you can commit to volunteering. Some roles may require a significant time commitment, while others are more flexible. Finding a role that fits your schedule and allows you to balance your other responsibilities is critical.
  3. **Skills and experience**. Consider your skills and experience and how they can be applied to the volunteer role. It will ensure that you can contribute meaningfully and leverage your strengths.
  4. **Organizational fit**. Finding a volunteer role that aligns with your values and goals is essential. Look for organizations with a mission that resonates with you and that you feel passionate about supporting.
  5. **Support and training**. Look for opportunities that offer support and training to help you develop new skills and succeed in your role. It will ensure you feel confident and prepared to make a meaningful impact.

Finding a volunteer role that aligns with your passions, skills, and goals is critical to making a meaningful impact and feeling fulfilled in your volunteer work. By considering these essential criteria, you can find a volunteer role that fits your needs and allows you to impact the world positively.

b. *What volunteer activities/projects do you recommend for people who are just starting to volunteer? And what about people who have been volunteering for a while?*

For people who are just beginning to volunteer, start with local community organizations or events. These can include food banks, shelters, or community cleanup projects. These volunteer activities are often short-term and require minimal training, making them a great way to start volunteering.

People who have volunteered for a while could benefit from more specialized volunteer opportunities that align with their skills and interests. For example, someone with a marketing background may consider volunteering for a nonprofit organization to help with their marketing and outreach efforts. Or, if someone is passionate about the environment, they may consider volunteering for a conservation organization to help with environmental research or advocacy.

In addition to specialized volunteer opportunities, I also recommend seeking leadership roles within volunteer organizations. It can include serving on a board of directors, leading a project or initiative, or mentoring other volunteers. These roles allow volunteers to develop their leadership skills and profoundly impact the organization and the community they serve.

Overall, the best volunteer activities and projects depend on the individual's skills, interests, and goals. By finding volunteer opportunities that align with these factors, volunteers can make a meaningful impact and feel fulfilled in their volunteer work.

  c. *How would you recommend planning a volunteering journey or building a*
     portfolio of volunteer activities?

Planning a volunteering journey or portfolio of volunteer activities can be a great way to demonstrate your commitment to positively impacting and showcasing your skills and experience to potential employers or other organizations. Here are some steps to consider when planning a volunteering journey or portfolio:

  1. **Set goals.** Start by setting goals for your volunteering journey. What do you want to achieve through your volunteer work? What skills or experience do you want to gain? Having clear goals will help you focus your efforts and make the most of your volunteer experiences.
  2. **Identify your skills and interests.** Consider your skills and interests and look for volunteer opportunities that align with them. It will ensure that you are engaged and motivated in your volunteer work and can make a meaningful impact.
  3. **Plan your volunteer activities.** Once you have identified potential volunteer opportunities, plan your volunteer activities to ensure you can make the most of your time and resources. Consider the time commitment, location, and any necessary training or preparation.
  4. **Reflect on your experiences.** After each volunteer activity, take the time to reflect on your experience. What did you learn? What skills did you develop? How did you make a positive impact? This reflection will help you identify growth and improvement areas and build on your successes.
  5. **Showcase your experiences.** Finally, showcase your volunteering journey or portfolio to others, such as potential employers or other organizations. It can be done through a resume or LinkedIn profile or by sharing your experiences in networking or interview settings.

By following these steps, volunteers can build a meaningful volunteering journey or portfolio demonstrating their commitment to positively impacting and showcasing their skills and experience to others.

The PMI KSA chapter slogan, "Together We Excel," is a powerful reminder of the importance of collaboration and teamwork in achieving our goals. It is especially true when it comes to volunteering, where volunteers often work together to positively impact our communities. Volunteers can achieve far more than ever by coming together and leveraging their collective skills, experiences, and resources.

Badr concludes:

> Whether volunteering as part of a team or collaborating with other organizations and volunteers, we can create a ripple effect of positive change that extends far beyond our efforts. So let us embrace the spirit of 'Together We Excel' and continue to work together towards a brighter future for all.

KEY TAKEAWAYS

- You should strategize your volunteer journey to help you define a learning path, just as you do for your professional career.
- Volunteer activities can be in various fields, such as finance, governance, communication, and partnerships.
- You should focus on activities to propel your career to project leadership.
- Types of roles, recognition, expected time commitment, and communication channels are all important criteria to consider.

YOUR A.H.A. MOMENT: ACTIVITY, HOPE, ACTION

It's your turn!

ACTIVITY

Answer the questions below:

- What skills do you want to learn? To improve?
- What activities can help you?
- What criteria are essential for you when you choose an activity?

HOPE

What activities do you hope to contribute to?
Prompt: "I hope to contribute to the following activities: ..."

ACTION

Write down one action to strategize your volunteering journey in the next three months.

11 How to Strategically Select the Right Role to Advance Your Career

Volunteering on a Board of Directors for a local industry association provided tremendous opportunities for me to advance my leadership skills. This volunteer role gave me access to leading teams, managing budgets and setting strategy. The all-volunteer board worked together without many of the pressures found in corporate settings.

Joe Pusz
President of the PMO Squad

In this chapter, we will guide you through these four typical volunteering roles in projectized organizations to help you choose the right one:

- contributor
- leader
- board member
- global volunteer

You will learn the benefits of each role and the valuable skills you can acquire in each of them, which you can then transfer to your career in project leadership. But before that, let's zoom out to understand the benefits of choosing your role strategically even in a volunteering setting.

LEARN TO CHOOSE YOUR NEXT VOLUNTEER ROLE

BEING STRATEGIC WILL KEEP YOU MOTIVATED AND FOCUSED

Some volunteers have stumbled by chance into volunteering: maybe they heard about it from a friend, decided to try it, and liked it. They volunteer for pleasure without considering a strategic plan for their volunteer career. Is this wrong? Not at all.

Other people have a clear strategy and set their sights on becoming a volunteer board member. Take Win*, a GenZ volunteer. He entered a new projectized organization and contributed to several different initiatives. He strove to be elected the best volunteer by lobbying. He asked about the requirements for becoming a board member in this projectized organization and was told that he needed three years of experience as a volunteer. Then, as soon as the three years had passed, Win began a real political campaign to become a board member, talking to other members and promoting himself on social media. Is this wrong? Not at all.

Being strategic about your volunteering journey can allow you to:

- remain motivated
- decline requests
- manage your energy and commitments

First, thinking about what you get from a volunteer role will help you remain motivated. Be clear about the reasons why you chose that role and write them down. When you feel less motivated, read your original motivations aloud to check if they have changed.

Second, it will help you to decline requests. When you volunteer in an organization, you may be contacted for help over and over again: "We need you for this event" or "What about hosting the next webinar?" And you may hesitate and finally accept because of the fear of missing out (FOMO). Aligning your volunteering experiences with your motivations and goals, as discussed in Chapter 10, will help you decline requests. For example, if you are gifted at writing articles, a friend of yours may ask you to write articles for a newsletter.

You have two roads here: you agree to do it because you enjoy writing articles even if you will not learn anything new, or you refuse it because you know it is more important to improve your speaking skills. There is no right or wrong answer, as long as you have fun doing the task. And thinking strategically will not remove the fun!

Lastly, if you strategize your journey, you have a compass to navigate the sea of endless possibilities and can manage your energy and commitments more effectively. You must concentrate on what you can achieve. The key is to choose meaningful yet realistic commitments, given your constraints.

How to Strategize Your Journey

Choosing the right volunteer opportunity requires proper consideration. You need to understand what you want and what the organization offers. Each volunteer role takes time, energy, and communication. Even if it is a short assignment, you'll interact with a new team, use collaborative tools, and get requests.

While enjoyment is paramount, aligning your skills, interests, and goals with the organization is also essential. If you want to consider your volunteering journey, answer the three questions below:

- Do I enjoy it here and now?
- What does this role bring to me in my volunteering journey?
- What does this role bring to me in my project leader career?

Your answers will give you insights into whether you want to remain in this role or move from your current position or organization.

To complement this strategy, you must know what the organization offers regarding volunteer roles and paths. If you are not yet part of the organization, check out their websites. Other volunteers may also share their stories with you.

Use your network. Do you have friends or acquaintances who volunteer in that organization? It may be time to send them a message. Regardless of whether you are currently inside or outside the organization, here are some questions you can ask:

- What are the different types of volunteer roles in this organization?
- What are the paths between these different roles?
- What are the eligibility requirements for each role?

Let's learn about different volunteer roles: contributor, team leader, board member, and global volunteer. You'll discover the benefits of each role, how to get that role, and the valuable skills you can acquire and transfer to your project leadership role.

VOLUNTEER ROLE 1: CONTRIBUTOR

In this role, you are not the leader of a volunteer team; you are part of a project team and contribute to the project, or perhaps you work alone. In any case, you don't make executive decisions or participate in strategic planning. However, you are a vital part of the projectized organization, as you will make things happen! As a contributor, you can focus on developing skills that are relevant to your career goal. You will get hands-on experience in a practical setting.

BENEFITS OF BEING A CONTRIBUTOR

As a contributor, you can have a well-defined, time-limited task. It can be an excellent way to start your volunteering journey if you are new to the organization or the volunteering world because you can understand what volunteering in that organization looks like. If you're an experienced volunteer within the organization, you might intentionally choose to serve as a contributor rather than a leader. For instance, perhaps you're keen on acquiring a new skill or gaining hands-on experience in a different activity. By stepping into a contributor role, you'll gain insights into the challenges faced by the team and challenge yourself to accept the role of a follower rather than a leader.

HOW TO BECOME A VOLUNTEER CONTRIBUTOR

Contributor roles are typical in organizations. They are not necessarily identified as "contributors," but the organization's description of their activities will help you to recognize these roles.

Let's take two examples. Jean-Luc* and Jessica* decided to take on an individual contributor volunteer role.

Situation 1: Jean-Luc is a program director leading technology projects. He wants to volunteer in an organization to learn more about accounting and finances. He volunteered as an individual contributor in a project where the organization needed to change all their charts of accounts.

Situation 2: Jessica has a few hours a month that she would like to dedicate to a projectized organization. She doesn't have a lot of time. She is applying for an individual contributor role, creating the slides for a board meeting.

As you can see, both Jean-Luc and Jessica have motivations or time constraints that prompt them to select a role as an individual contributor. Both of them are thinking strategically.

Skills You Can Transfer to Your Project Leader Role

You are a project leader at work: you are used to leading, organizing, and driving change. It's not easy to accept that you're no longer in the driver's seat. As Francesca Gino recommends, we must teach people to lead and follow.[1] This is what she calls flexing. And it's an excellent way to learn about yourself.

Being a contributor develops your empathy. You must be patient in the face of change and accept the team's pace, even if it is not your own pace. If you disagree with the direction taken, you must refrain from trying to assume a leadership role yourself.

Volunteers' Stories: Yahaira Perez Jose in the USA

Yahaira Perez Jose is volunteering in the professional development team at the PMI Northern Utah chapter. She joined looking to increase her network and community contribution. Inspired by others' initiatives, she stepped into a contributor role. She said, "Volunteering transformed my routine, offering challenges and growth opportunities that make the experience more rewarding." In her role, she engages speakers and organizes monthly events. It pushed her to improve her networking skills, gain valuable organizational insights, and practice other skills that she does not get to use frequently in her regular job. "Volunteering has boosted my confidence and fulfillment. I've also discovered that volunteering is more than giving back; it's building meaningful connections and finding purpose."

VOLUNTEER ROLE 2: TEAM LEADER

As a team leader, you can either manage a team or lead a project team. Taking on a leadership role in the volunteering setting can be very valuable when you aspire to a management or leadership position in your career development.

Benefits of Being a Team Leader

Being a team leader in a volunteer setting is a valuable experience for those who may not have people reporting directly to them in their professional roles. While you will not have the responsibility of managing vacations, bonuses, and other workplace perks, you will face a unique challenge. You'll need to improve your ability to inspire and coordinate individuals without traditional hierarchical authority. If you are already a team leader at work, you must be even more influential, negotiate more, and build stronger relationships, because volunteers can jump ship whenever they want. The findings of two empirical studies on a sample of volunteers in the nonprofit sector have shown that leaders of volunteers need to provide the following[2]:

- structure and clarity about roles and responsibilities
- consideration and recognition

Another study comparing volunteers and employees performing the same job tasks has shed light on the fact that social interactions are more important for volunteers than for employees.[3]

By learning to provide these things for your volunteer team, you will improve your leadership abilities and have the opportunity to experiment and improve as a team leader.

How to Become a Volunteer Team Leader

The path to this role may vary depending on the organization. Enquire about the requirements to become a leader in the organization:

- Do you need to have been a member of the organization for several years?
- Do you need to have been an active contributor for a certain number of years?

The size and impact of teams and projects may be different. Be clear about what you can contribute. Here are two situations you may encounter.

Situation 1: You are the leader of a newly created volunteer team.

You will need to do the job while hiring new volunteers. Together you will build a strategy and pave the way to delivering outcomes.

Pros: You can decide who should join the team.

Cons: You might need to handle a heavy workload while the team is growing and training. It can be arduous if you are also new to the organization, because you will be on your own learning path.

Situation 2: You are the leader of an existing team.

Be sure to talk with the volunteers who are already in place before accepting the role. It will help you find out whether you can get on well with the team. You will also identify what has been done so far and the challenges they have encountered. You can then envision how you can help them.

Once you accept this role, you must become a learner and get familiar with the existing tools and processes. Chat with the volunteers to uncover the unwritten rules and procedures. You will discover gaps and areas for improvement. But don't be too quick to change things. Assess how resistant the organization and your team are to change. Don't immediately criticize the way things are done. Things can be done differently and still work even if they are not done your way. Sometimes, when someone takes up a leadership role, after a few months, they are praised for having restructured everything. The volunteers who made valuable contributions to the team before the leader arrived may feel hurt, as it implies they didn't do a good job before the new leader arrived.

Pros: Volunteers in the existing team can help you from day one.

Cons: You must fit in with existing processes that you had no part in creating. Some volunteers may leave.

Skills You Can Transfer to Your Project Leader Role

Whether in a volunteer setting or at work, leading means laying out a strategy, inspiring people, and helping them to grow. Being a volunteer leader will build or reinforce your leadership experiences.

While you volunteer, take some time to think about what you are learning:

- How did I encourage some team members to contribute more?
- How did I build a great team?
- How did I feel when I couldn't do everything I wanted?

The other interesting challenge you can experience in the volunteer setting is the high turnover of human resources, which forces you to organize backup or transfer knowledge in a systematic way. Note that volunteer teams also follow the four stages of Tuckman's team development model. If there is considerable turnover, volunteer teams will spend longer in the forming stage and can't progress easily to the performing stage.[4]

Think about how you can transfer your volunteer learning to the workplace.

Does everything collapse when you are not here? Perhaps you should share more information and knowledge with your team.

Are you the only person prepared to roll up your sleeves? Are you always the person who finds solutions to problems? Perhaps you should share the burden with your team.

VOLUNTEERS' STORIES: AYANDA NYIKANA IN SOUTH AFRICA

Ayanda Nyikana is a seasoned contributor to the PMI South Africa chapter as the senior vice president for Rising Leaders. "I want to do good for others and the community," she told us. And she doesn't spare her efforts. She has a team and leads three portfolios – Academic Outreach, Social Impact, and Early Career Professionals. In her leadership role, she oversees several projects. She added, "Seeing a project from concept to complete execution most certainly brings fulfillment, and you can see your work in concrete form. It motivates one to do more and inspire others to be involved."

There are many benefits she has gained through her engagement. She can learn from others, create authentic and lifelong relationships, and make a difference in someone's life.

She concluded:

> Whatever task you take on, you are accountable for it and ensure it's fulfilling. On the road to achieving your goals, you must apply discipline but, most importantly, consistency because without commitment, you'll never start, and without consistency, you never finish. Volunteering shouldn't be a chore or a job; when you can share your time with others, make sure it's done in a way that feels right to others and helps you utilize your best to help others be their best.

VOLUNTEER ROLE 3: BOARD MEMBER

As a board member, you must steer the organization's strategy. You make decisions about the future of the organization and contribute to its vision. You also follow the organization's ethical, legal, and financial management policies.

BENEFITS OF BEING A BOARD MEMBER

Volunteering as a board member offers a remarkable leadership opportunity. You will network at a higher level with community or industry governance experts, and you can explore whether a future top management leadership role at work is something you will enjoy.

We anonymously surveyed 30 worldwide volunteer board members at the PMI to gather deeper insights. Some participants who had volunteered as chapter board members for less than three years did not have a previous role within the organization. However, they still found value in their volunteer experience, such as improving their communication skills and gaining courage in their daily lives. One respondent said, "Volunteering as a board member – vice president of membership – is challenging for me. It's like a growing path, giving me courage in my daily life and work."

Those who had volunteered for three to five years reported varying experiences. Some had previous roles within the organization, such as being involved in outreach or serving as the program director for a community. One respondent highlighted how volunteering helped them work effectively with teams in their volunteer role and at work. Another individual explained, "Being bolder, speaking up more, expressing myself, and listening to others were skills I developed through my board membership."

Respondents with more extensive board experience, both 5–10 years and 10+ years, emphasized the benefits of volunteering in leadership development, networking, and professional recognition. They mentioned gaining valuable insights by contributing to the thought process, building global contacts, and becoming subject matter experts. One respondent pointed out how managing a team of volunteers taught them essential people management skills.

Antonio Nieto-Rodriguez served as the chair of the PMI Board of Directors. Here's what he shared with us:

> I learned that the two most important tasks of any major role are a) crafting a compelling vision for PMI that unites us all; b) creating a high-performing team – don't assume that this will happen naturally, it is hard work.

How to Become a Volunteer Board Member

The way to become a board member can vary between organizations and chapters. It is crucial to review each organization's specific requirements and guidelines carefully. Some skills or work-related experience are also required. As a volunteer board member, you will be responsible for a particular domain or team, like finance, governance, partnership, technology, or communication.

If you aspire to serve on a board, here are a few recommendations:

- It is best to start volunteering in some way for the organization before applying for the board position.
- You must know the organization's processes, bylaws, and working methods.
- You should be familiar with the different teams and their roles.

To be a great board member, you should showcase your commitment and reliability. Embrace accountability and demonstrate strong problem-solving skills. Following these steps will prepare you for a board position, through which you can positively impact the organization.

Let's review two situations:

Situation 1: Daniel* has volunteered as a project leader in a cultural organization for the last two years. His projects have been successful. He is familiar with the organization, the teams, and the processes. He learned about an open position on the board that relates to his job experience. He decided to apply. He enjoys the board position and can confidently participate in all activities and tasks.

Situation 2: Nycol* is a newbie project manager. She just got the Project Management Professional (PMP) certification and decided to volunteer for a projectized organization. She found a board position and applied. Her previous experience fitted with the role. However, after a few months, she was feeling overwhelmed by the pressure to learn all the processes and procedures, missing deadlines, and needing help in meetings. The team tried to help and mentor her, but she realized it wasn't the right moment for her to volunteer as a board member.

Both situations are extreme: one is smooth and easy, and the other is more challenging. You need to self-assess whether you are ready for a board position. If you are, go for it!

Skills You Can Transfer to Your Project Leader Role

Volunteering as a board member provides valuable opportunities to transfer skills and experiences to your daily work. This is true regardless of whether you are a project leader exposed to budgets and strategic planning or a new project coordinator in your paid job. Overcoming challenges like communication issues, lack of resources, lack of engagement, and managing exit interviews requires proactive leadership skills that you can apply in the workplace.

Our survey of board members also revealed the positive impact of volunteering on careers, such as securing better roles in different companies, earning respect and recognition, and gaining advantages in job interviews. It also highlighted how volunteering as a board member can shape and enhance careers.

Volunteers' Stories: Mazin Gadir in the UAE

Mazin Gadir is a seasoned volunteer board member and a strategy and innovation expert in the healthcare industry. He first began as a volunteer in the outreach team at the PMI UAE chapter. He liked it very much and was mentored by other volunteers. When the board election occurred, he seized the opportunity and became a board member. Since then, he has become a genuine advocate for volunteering. Here are just three of the countless benefits that he identified.

First, he learned the secrets of servant leadership and humility. As a board member, he looked after several volunteers, which is a heavy responsibility. Some people can become distracted by the status, visibility, and exposure provided by the board member role. But Mazin keeps a cool head despite his success and leadership position.

> Being a board director makes you a volunteer with extra serving capabilities. You are much more of a servant than a normal volunteer is. The only difference between a board director and a normal volunteer is that now, as a board director, you serve more than yourself. You serve, inspire and nurture others.

Second, he has learned how to negotiate, conduct critical conversations, and handle other people's ideas with diplomacy. He has improved his listening skills a lot.

Third, his role has broadened his knowledge. As a board member, he took part in several events and conferences. He got to learn about the banking sector, the construction sector, the telecom sector, and aviation. "I enjoy volunteering, taking the lessons learned from one industry and seeing how they apply in healthcare. And vice versa."

On the personal side, he has expanded his network dramatically, and he picked up several mentors and coaches outside of his industry because of his volunteering activities.

Serving the community is truly what motivates Mazin. He has also taken up a new board role in the PMO Leader community.

VOLUNTEER ROLE 4: GLOBAL VOLUNTEER

A global volunteer engages in a volunteer role in projects or initiatives that cross geographical boundaries and have an impact beyond local communities or local chapters.

BENEFITS OF BEING A GLOBAL VOLUNTEER

You'll develop your international skills, cultural awareness, and visibility in this role. Depending on your role, you may find yourself at the heart of the organization's changes and adaptations to coming trends. Global volunteers can also constitute a pool of volunteers who can help with other initiatives or one-off projects.

HOW TO BECOME A GLOBAL VOLUNTEER

Being a global volunteer in a projectized organization can take different forms. Here are some examples of roles:

- translating standards and certifications
- reviewing proposals for conferences
- participation in events to manage a forum
- managing social media for a global event
- being part of the team organizing an international conference or webinar
- global mentoring

Other roles include more extended involvement, like being part of insights teams, being a facilitator, or managing transversal projects.

Find out how it works in the organization that you would like to volunteer for, and check whether you need to have a specific background (such as holding a leadership role or being an executive in your day job) or whether you need to have served for several years in the organization.

SKILLS YOU CAN TRANSFER TO YOUR PROJECT LEADER ROLE

As a global volunteer, you can understand how strategy is defined or evolved based on members' and customers' needs or geopolitical situations. You can strengthen your strategic thinking skills. As a project leader, developing the big picture helps you to see new perspectives and solutions. One particular skill that global volunteering will give you is cultural fluency: the ability to collaborate with people worldwide; this is a true treasure that no book can replace. You can apply what you learn to your day job as an international project leader. If you don't work in global teams, this volunteer experience will enrich your skill palette for a future role.

VOLUNTEERS' STORIES: RAJI SIVARAMAN IN SINGAPORE

Raji Sivaraman, principal, pracademic (a practitioner and an academic), is a lifelong volunteer. Volunteering is part of her family DNA. If she can help anyone, she does so, no matter what. Over the years, she has volunteered at PMI, PMOGA, IPMA, AWWA (Asian Women's Welfare Association), the UN, WAFA (Water Air Food Awards), Agile Alliance, and various musical organizations. For her, becoming a global volunteer was a natural path: "I speak many languages; I travel a lot, and I can assimilate with many geographies and cultures. I love learning new languages, cultures, and working methods." Through her global volunteer roles, she honed many skills like communication, public speaking, finance, and IT. To her, continuous learning and transferable skills are just a mindset you need to engage your brain so that you can work how you want, whether in everyday life, your job, or a volunteer role.

Raji concludes, "I can never stop as it is part of my every breath. Volunteering is my zen zone, and I love all the people and organizations I volunteer for."

CASE STUDY: WHAT IF I LEARN LESS THAN I EXPECTED?

Maria* is a software developer in a big corporation. She experiences a lot of stress at work. Since she started volunteering, she has noticed she feels better. She has volunteered for three years as a website administrator in a medium-sized not-for-profit. She enjoys volunteering there because she considers the other volunteers as her friends. Debbie*, the director of the small not-for-profit, is very grateful to Maria. She tells her, "We hope you will stay in this role for a long time. We had difficulties finding a volunteer for the website; you are reliable and competent. We are grateful to you." Maria has sometimes canceled friends' appointments because of her volunteering commitments, and her friends have often told her: "You spent hours doing this activity for free and for years. What's the point? Do you learn a lot?" She hadn't thought about this before, and it made her think. Should she give up her role and look for another one? There will be board elections in the not-for-profit. She never applied before, because she likes what she does on the website and does not enjoy politics. At work, she would want to apply for a leadership role. So, a board position could help her gain confidence. On the other hand, she feels bad about letting Debbie down by moving to another role. Debbie relies on her.

What should Maria do? Should she go on volunteering as a web administrator or apply for a board position?

Our Views

Maria loves volunteering as a website administrator in this small not-for-profit because she knows the work well, has made good friends there, and finds it fun. Since she started volunteering, she feels her well-being has improved.

We recommend that Maria undertake a quick analysis, as follows:

- What she likes: website administration and working with friends
- What she doesn't like: politics and inaction

Maria should also reach out to current board members to find out what they do, what they enjoy, and what challenges they face. She can then understand better how being a board member helped them in their volunteering journey.

In light of this, she can write down the pros and cons of the website administrator role and the board member role. Then, she can make sound decisions with the gathered data and listen to her gut.

VOLUNTEERS' STORIES: BRIGITTE SCHADEN IN AUSTRIA

Brigitte Schaden is an Austrian senior manager, consultant, coach, and business mediator. She has a mathematician background and began her career as a project manager. She took part in the events of the Austrian Project Management Association. She also got IPMA certifications. One day, in the late 90s, she began her volunteering journey. "I was interested in the certification system, and I wanted to contribute to further developments," she told us. Curiosity pushed Brigitte to embark on volunteering. In Austria, volunteering is quite common. She has been volunteering for more than 25 years. She occupied different roles: controller, board member, chair of the board, chair of the council, and president of the IPMA. Being the president of the IPMA was hard work: "I was working 6.5 days per week. Starting with Sunday lunch, my free time started, and it was over on Monday morning. That was tough."

One of the aspects of volunteering that Brigitte wanted to highlight is her experience as a board member. Being a board member requires specific skills. It is essential to have a broad vision of the whole organization to initiate innovations. Leadership skills are also crucial. "It means creating good working conditions for everyone to have fun and to be able to work autonomously," she added. Looking back, thanks to her volunteering experiences, she gained invaluable skills like negotiation, persuasion, using informal power, active listening, including all sides, considering the views of all parties involved and giving them space, and learning to make compromises.

In addition, she explained, "Through contact with so many different cultures, my field of vision has broadened. It makes you realize that there are very different solutions to problems and not always just 'the one.' You get an excellent international network."

When she moved to consulting, she could better serve her customers using her international expertise and knowledge of global project management standards.

The lectures she gave worldwide increased her competence and personal brand. But above all, volunteering has created long-lasting friendships.

"Volunteering in a projectized organization can be a lot of fun, hard work, and joy in helping to shape the organization you are volunteering in. You can build up a personal, broad network that you can fall back on again and again," she concluded.

KEY TAKEAWAYS

- Strategizing your volunteering journey can help you remain motivated and find your next exciting role.
- Review the role description carefully and talk with the organization before engaging in a volunteer role to ensure the role will align with your career goals.
- There are different possible journeys and opportunities: contributor, leader, board member, and global volunteer. All of them have challenges and benefits.

YOUR A.H.A. MOMENT: ACTIVITY, HOPE, ACTION

It's your turn!

ACTIVITY

Answer the questions below:

- Can you say "No" to volunteer roles? Why or why not?
- Can you list the different types of volunteer roles in the organization where you volunteer?
- What roles would you like to take on during your volunteer journey? Why?

HOPE

What role do you wish to reach in the long term in your volunteering journey?
Prompt: "By volunteering, I hope to become..."

ACTION

In the next three months, reach out to one volunteer in the role you wish to reach in the long term.

NOTES

1 Gino, D. F. (2019, November–December). Cracking the Code of Sustained Collaboration. *Harvard Business Review Magazine*. https://hbr.org/2019/11/cracking-the-code-of-sustained-collaboration

2 Schreiner, E., Trent, S. B., Prange, K. A., & Allen, J. A. (2018). Leading volunteers: Investigating volunteers' perceptions of leaders' behavior and gender. *Nonprofit Management and Leadership*, 29(2), 241–260. https://onlinelibrary.wiley.com/doi/abs/10.1002/nml.21331

3 Pearce, J. L. (1983). Job attitude and motivation differences between volunteers and employees from comparable organizations. *Journal of Applied Psychology*, 68(4), 646–652. https://psycnet.apa.org/doiLanding?doi=10.1037%2F0021-9010.68.4.646

4 Tuckman, B. W. (1965). Developmental sequence in small groups. *Psychological Bulletin*, 63(6), 384–399. https://doi.org/10.1037/h0022100. PMID 14314073

12 Further Considerations about Volunteering

Volunteering gives you a better understanding of the community of practice and gives you a sense of purpose outside your regular job. Overall, volunteering represents a unique and significant way to support one's work and career goals.

Joel Carboni
Founder of Green Project Management (GPM)

In this chapter, we will give you some advice and answers to common questions to make the most of your volunteering journey. Here are the topics we will cover:

- partnering with another volunteer to enhance the experience
- dealing with a toxic environment
- how to fully understand your role
- taking on multiple opportunities
- how to make changes in an organization
- deciding how long to volunteer for
- preparing your exit

PARTNERING WITH ANOTHER VOLUNTEER TO ENHANCE THE EXPERIENCE

To maximize the benefits of the volunteer experience, you can find a role model, a buddy, or a mentor within the organization you're going to join:

- A role model is someone you admire, are inspired by, and want to emulate.
- A buddy, who has a role similar to yours, guides you by answering any questions you may have about the role.
- A mentor is someone you can ask questions and consult when you have doubts.

These people will ease your onboarding and integration into the role. You can reach out to them whenever you need to. They will also provide a psychologically safe place where you can open up.

During your volunteering journey, you should monitor how you are feeling about the project you are participating in. Consider these simple questions to evaluate your needs:

 DOI: 10.1201/9781003407942-15

- Do I enjoy volunteering here? Why?
- What do I want to get from volunteering here?
- Do my goals still align with the project volunteer role?

DEALING WITH A TOXIC ENVIRONMENT

As you already know, project volunteering means delivering projects sometimes under tight deadlines and with limited resources – and with no compensation. And sometimes, you may find yourself trapped in a toxic environment. But what's a toxic environment?

In a study, Donald Sull and his colleagues identified five attributes of a toxic culture: it is disrespectful, non-inclusive, unethical, cutthroat, and abusive.[1] These attributes can help you identify whether you are in a toxic culture.

If so, run! But before looking for the exit, take a moment to reflect on the source of the toxicity. Is it an individual problem, limited to certain people you work with? Or is it a systemic issue within the organization itself? Dive deep into the matter and identify where the problem lies.

Don't go down the gossip route if the toxicity arises from specific individuals. Instead, escalate the matter to higher levels of authority within the projectized organization. Take a proactive approach to managing the situation by focusing on concrete facts and evidence. Seek out someone who can provide support and guidance through the process.

However, if you discover the toxicity is deeply rooted in the organization's culture and practices, then it's time to run. Recognize that some environments are beyond repair; the best action is to distance yourself from the toxicity.

INTERVIEW WITH ELIZABETH BORCIA ON TOXIC ENVIRONMENTS

We have interviewed Elizabeth Borcia, an organizational psychologist, on toxic environments.

a. *Are there toxic environments in the volunteering space?*

At the end of the day, people are people. The exact psychological and social mechanisms that lead to toxic behavior in the workplace are responsible for toxic behavior in volunteer environments. We constantly hear about toxic work environments and bad managers in the corporate world. Thus, finding parallel organizations in the nonprofit sector should be familiar to everyone. There may be more toxicity in volunteer organizations because the talent pool is reduced – top performers gravitate towards busy careers with high compensation, not volunteer positions. The idiom "beggars can't be choosers" comes to mind.

b. *How do you handle a toxic environment in a volunteering setting?*

The best action for dealing with a toxic environment may be to leave it. Still, one benefit to staying in a toxic environment may be strengthening your psychological resilience and emotional intelligence. These concepts involve regulating emotions (e.g., frustration, sadness, embarrassment) when faced with challenges, such as working with a "difficult" co-worker or manager. They are difficult soft skills to teach but are vital leadership skills – the absence of which is responsible for many toxic environments in the first place. A volunteer environment may provide the rare opportunity to practice in a low-stakes environment, unattached from your income or personal relationships. For example, it is considerably easier to shrug off exorbitant criticism from a short-term volunteer project manager than from your full-time boss (or mother-in-law). However, don't think you, a lone volunteer, will change a toxic culture. It is well established in the academic literature that cultural change must begin with "top-down" leadership (the board of directors, executive director, etc.). Expecting others to change, rather than focusing on your skill development, will only lead to frustration, disappointment, and burnout. I advise anyone volunteering in a toxic environment to do a cost–benefit analysis. Are the expected gains (e.g., resume experience, new skills, personal fulfillment, etc.) worth the drawbacks (e.g., added stress, longer hours, less free time, etc.)? Only stay in the toxic environment if you have the cognitive resources to handle it. Be realistic, and don't be a hero for the cause.

HOW TO FULLY UNDERSTAND YOUR ROLE

According to one definition:

> Role ambiguity is present when volunteers do not understand how an organization works, do not understand how to cater to the service beneficiaries, and do not know how to seek support to complete their job according to the assigned responsibilities.[2]

The volunteer role can be ambiguous regarding tasks, responsibilities, or deadlines. We've seen that role ambiguity is a potential source of conflict. Still, role ambiguity can have other harmful effects:

- You can be stressed because you need help understanding what to do and what to deliver.
- You can be demotivated because you don't know who to ask for help.
- Your contribution may not be needed.
- You may feel frustrated because this lack of clarity impacts your personal time.

We recommend you talk with the volunteers' manager to explain the impacts on your life and well-being and ask for more clarity.

TAKING ON MULTIPLE OPPORTUNITIES

Check if the organization allows you to participate in different activities or roles. Some organizations do not allow people to have simultaneous roles within or outside the organization because of the risk of conflicts of interest or excessive workload. During your journey, you may also be asked to take on an additional role because of your expertise, passion, and commitment, or because people like collaborating with you.

Ask yourself these two questions:

- What will you gain from each opportunity?
- Can you manage it all?

If you want to take on the new role (and you are allowed to), set a trial period. Be transparent by informing the teams you belong to that you'd like to evaluate the workload by trying out the new role for a certain number of weeks. From there, you can understand what is required and whether you can cope with it.

HOW TO MAKE CHANGES IN AN ORGANIZATION

In the volunteering world, people have scarce time and resources. You may arrive with big dreams: transform an organization, establish new practices you couldn't apply in your day job, or instigate radical change. But as the first few weeks pass by, you encounter resistance. "We have done it this way for years." "This is not the priority." You ask questions, but the answers do not come. You propose ideas, and no one buys in. You begin to be discouraged.

We have experienced this ourselves. Resistance to change may come from the organization or from individuals. Or perhaps the turnover is high in the organization, and this instability does not foster deep discussions about change. Be patient, listen, learn how the organization works and how the teams can collaborate better, and then propose the change. You can also apply for a board role to drive the strategy and bring about change.

DECIDING HOW LONG TO VOLUNTEER FOR

Learning a skill or modeling a behavior takes time, practice, and effort. Your choice of how long to volunteer for depends on the reasons why you volunteer in this projectized organization. A short assignment will work if you are aiming to get some contacts or participate in an event. However, you must contribute to a longer-term project if you want to impact your community and improve your skills. Advertised volunteer roles usually indicate their duration: sometimes there is a one-year minimum, sometimes two years. This is deliberate. Volunteering requires commitment. You need to build relationships with stakeholders to make things happen – and it may take more time because you are not a full-time employee in the organization.

PREPARING YOUR EXIT

You may need to move on to another volunteer role at a certain point. Change is a natural part of life, whether due to new job commitments, shifting interests, or other personal or professional activities. You always need to be ready to prepare for your exit. Some organizations rely heavily on volunteers, so if you disappear, it will

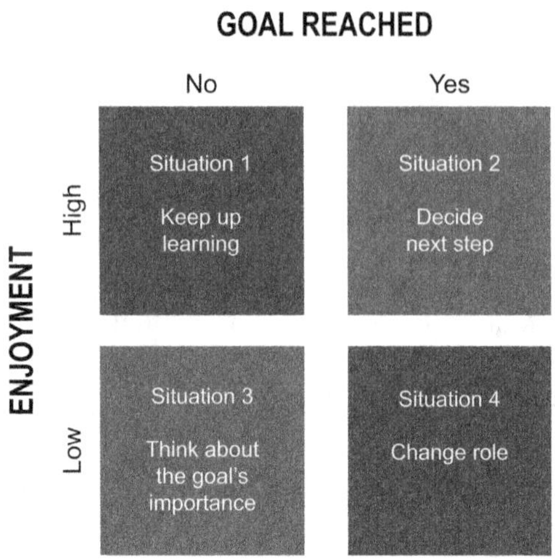

GOAL REACHED

FIGURE 12.1   Exit Criteria: Goal Reached and Enjoyment Level

impact your colleagues' workload and some projects' outcomes. That is why we want to talk specifically about exit preparation.

How to Know You Have to Exit

It's good to have some alarms set or exit criteria from the outset.

⊟ You can write them in My Volunteering Canvas.
Here are some possible exit criteria:

- I don't enjoy it anymore.
- I'm not learning anymore.
- The role has changed.
- I'm bored.
- I don't have time.
- I don't bring value.
- I don't align anymore with the values of the organization.
- I'm exhausted.
- My friends in the organization have left.

Here are four different situations you might face; these are illustrated in Figure 12.1.

Situation 1: You have not reached your goal, and you still enjoy volunteering. So it makes sense to continue until you achieve your goal.

Situation 2: You have reached your goal, and you still enjoy volunteering. It is up to you whether to stay or leave.

Situation 3: You have not reached your goal, but volunteering has become a source of stress. Do you decide to exit even if your goal has not been achieved? How important is this goal for you? Can you pursue the same goal in another role or another organization?

Situation 4: You have reached your goal, but volunteering is **not as enjoyable as it used to be or no longer provides additional benefits**. You should consider your engagement.

Mayte's volunteer journey as a local TEDx event organizer was filled with passion and dedication. However, there came a moment when she paused, thought hard, and realized that after six incredible years, it was time to step down. The volunteer opportunity had been a cherished part of her life, providing abundant knowledge and personal and professional growth. However, she acknowledged the need to prioritize her family and other commitments.

At first, she felt slightly unsure, but bravely recognized that her interests were changing. She embraced the idea that it was time to move on and let go of her role.

Once she decided to go, she communicated properly with the organization, expressed gratitude for the experience, and offered her assistance for a smooth transition to the new team member. Mayte still cherishes the memories, the friends, and the fantastic moments shared in the organization.

ANTICIPATE YOUR EXIT

As Stephen Covey wrote in his best-selling book, *The Seven Habits of Highly Effective People*, "Start with the end in mind."[3] It's better to prepare for your exit along the way. Just because volunteering is unpaid doesn't mean you can drop everything and walk out. You can still behave professionally and respectfully and transfer the knowledge properly.

Volunteering has fewer constraints than work when you want to leave, but you also have less time to prepare the necessary documentation. That's why we recommend you prepare along the way. A well-organized exit will contribute to your good reputation.

Think honestly about the end of your journey:

- How do you want to be remembered?
- What legacy do you want to leave?
- Will you feel happy if everything collapses when you go?

These are questions that transcend your ego.

The following are essential steps to incorporate into your exit strategy:

- Check if the organization has an exit process you need to follow.
- Inform them that you are going to leave.
- Prepare and finalize the handover.
- Express your gratitude.
- Confirm if you are happy to be contacted in the future or not.

Here are three possible situations you may face when you want to prepare your handover and some thoughts on how to handle them.

Situation 1: Your successor is known and belongs to the same organization.

In this case, your task is more straightforward. You are both part of the same organization, so you already share a common language, which will save you time.

Schedule regular check-ins (depending on the amount of time between your decision to leave and your actual exit) to explain the context of the role, the struggles you faced, and the further work you have envisioned. Your successor will not necessarily face the same challenges as you did, but the information is still useful.

Situation 2: **Your successor is known and does not belong to the same organization.**

You must check when your successor will arrive, what information can be shared in advance, and the organization's confidentiality rules. You must also decide if you will be available to help when they take up the role.

Situation 3: **Your successor is unknown.**

In this case, you will need to prepare more detailed information. The information can be in the form of documents, short videos, or memos. Again, you need to confirm whether you can support your successor.

CASE STUDY: SHOULD I STOP THIS VOLUNTEERING ROLE?

Raquel* has been volunteering for three years in a projectized organization. She is passionate about it. However, lately, she has been feeling overwhelmed whenever she receives a new request or message from her volunteer peers. Though she still responds professionally, she notices that it drains her energy. Raquel enjoys it less than before. There is a professional development event coming up, and the board asks if Raquel wants to manage it. It is a sign of trust, but Raquel hesitates. She doesn't have the heart to commit to a year of preparation for this event. She also wonders about her future in this organization.

Should she accept the request to manage the event?

OUR VIEWS

We advise Raquel not to accept the position. Raquel should review whether she is in an appropriate organization, performing an activity she enjoys, and supporting her volunteer SMART (Specific, Measurable, Achievable, Realistic, and Time-bound) goals. We recommend taking a break or reducing her volunteering engagement; that will help her review her volunteer goals and decide the best option.

VOLUNTEERS' STORIES: PAUL OKEOGHENE OMUGBE IN NIGERIA

"I decided to volunteer because I wanted to be part of a professional community where I could give back. I also wanted to be in a society that would help me get another certification besides my accounting certifications," said Paul Okeoghene Omugbe, business and project director in a start-up management consulting company in Nigeria.

He is a past president of the PMI Nigeria chapter, which has over 2,000 members. "One of the principles that I live by is that I should be able to create value and be of value anywhere I find myself." And that is what he tries to achieve in his volunteering activities.

Volunteering has helped him build his leadership and communication skills. He has to deal with various stakeholders from various generations, roles, and professional experiences. It can be daunting sometimes.

Second, he has to be diplomatic, objective, and strategic while carrying everyone along.

> For example, not everyone will buy into your strategy, but you must try as much as you can to get the buy-in of a majority of the board through a voting process and try to implement strategies that will stand the test of time.

When there are new strategies to execute, it is essential to talk with volunteers to convince them. Reflecting on his volunteering journey, Paul cannot overemphasize the importance of teamwork. For him, it means allowing everyone to express their ideas and develop their initiatives. Paul communicates the objective clearly to the other volunteers and enables them to accomplish the goal using their own initiative. "You cannot succeed in leading a volunteer group or community by micromanaging your team. You must be a servant leader and allow the team to learn and grow." Mindset is crucial when learning your role in an organization. It's not about titles. It's about giving value and giving your best to impact other people's lives positively.

For Paul, volunteering will never stop, because volunteering in a projectized organization is one of the most prestigious ways of giving back as a project manager.

And, we cannot agree more with Paul's last message: "Project management is not just a profession but a life skill."

KEY TAKEAWAYS

- Partner with another volunteer to maximize the benefits of your volunteering journey.
- You might be in a toxic environment, which may strengthen your resilience, but don't be a hero; leave it. You don't need to demonstrate anything to anyone!
- Role ambiguity is a common issue in volunteering; talking with your manager will help clarify the expectations and boundaries.
- You may want to take on multiple roles; set up a trial period to evaluate whether you can commit in the longer term.
- You may experience resistance to change: Be patient, listen, then propose changes.
- Try to stick with an activity long enough to learn and practice some new skills.
- Always be ready to prepare for your exit by documenting and transferring knowledge, which will ease the handover.

YOUR A.H.A. MOMENT: ACTIVITY, HOPE, ACTION

It's your turn!

ACTIVITY

Answer the three questions below:

- What are your exit criteria?
- What two actions can you perform in preparation for your exit from volunteering?
- How can you manage toxic environments?

HOPE

What do you hope to leave as a legacy when you exit a volunteering role?
Prompt: "When I exit my volunteer role, I hope …"

ACTION

Write down one action you can take to improve your handover in case you leave your volunteer role.

NOTES

1 Sull, D., Sull, C., Cipolli, W., & Brighenti, C. (2022, March). Why Every Leader Needs to Worry about Toxic Culture. *MIT Sloan Management Review.* https://sloanreview.mit.edu/article/why-every-leader-needs-to-worry-about-toxic-culture/
2 Purwanto, B. M., & Rostiani, R. (2022, October). The Influence of Enthusiasm and Personal Constraints on the Intention to Continue Volunteering in an Uncertain and Turbulent Environment. *International Review on Public and Nonprofit Marketing.* https://link.springer.com/article/10.1007/s12208-022-00349-z
3 Franklin Covey. (n.d.). Habit 2: Begin with the End in Mind. https://www.franklincovey-benelux.com/fr/resources/habit-2-begin-with-the-end-in-mind/#:~:text=Habit%20 2%3A%20Begin%20With%20the%20End%20in%20Mind%20means%20 to,always%20in%20the%20right%20direction.

13 Conclusion
How to Bring Your New Learning Back into Your Project Career

The problems we face today come at us so fast, and are so complex, that we need groups of talented people to tackle them, led by gifted leaders, or even teams of leaders.[1]

Warren Bennis

In this final chapter, you will explore how your volunteering journey can contribute to honing your leadership skills, developing your network, and exploring new fields, ultimately supporting your journey to becoming a project leader, regardless of your career level.

You must develop the appropriate mindset and reflect on your volunteering experiences to integrate what you have learned into your professional life.

DEVELOP THE RIGHT MINDSET

As a project leader, you have embarked on a lifelong learning journey. This learning journey might be challenging. You will not know everything, you will make mistakes, and you may experience failures along the way. But ultimately you can be successful if you have the right mindset. You need to accept that:

- Not knowing everything will encourage you to ask more questions.
- Making mistakes is part of the learning process.
- Failures are part of your success.

You cannot improve all your skills at the same time. To use a sports analogy: don't try to win multiple races simultaneously. You might be overwhelmed and discouraged by your lack of progress. Pick one or two things you need to develop and concentrate on them. Have clear goals and objectives to set yourself on the right path for success.

PAUSE AND REFLECT

Throughout your volunteering journey, you will have fun, but you will sometimes struggle, and you might even question your involvement. Take the time to pause and reflect. You can review My Volunteering Canvas and ask your support network

DOI: 10.1201/9781003407942-16

to give you new perspectives on your challenges. Review the tools, techniques, and A.H.A. (Activity, Hope, Action) moments provided in the previous chapters. And remember, you can also integrate what you have learned into your day job.

Here are a few questions that can help you in the process of reflection:

- How does this volunteer activity relate to my career development goals as a project leader?
- What did I learn?
- What are my pain points or struggles?

DEVELOP YOUR LEADERSHIP SKILLS

As a project leader, you need to hone your leadership skills. To begin, it's essential to identify which leadership skills you want to develop or improve. Early in your career, you may focus on acquiring technical or communication skills and learning different leadership styles.

Regardless of your age or experience, you can enhance your project leadership skill set as a new project leader. Some volunteers we spoke with hadn't held formal project leadership roles yet. However, they were actively honing their leadership skills through volunteering.

For seasoned project leaders, the emphasis may shift to mastering and refining skills. Taking on leadership or board member roles can prepare you for future positions within your workplace, while opting for a contributor role will help you to remain adaptable.

For each skill, it is essential to assess where you stand. With the knowledge and practice acquired through volunteering, ask yourself these questions:

- How can I excel in the leadership skills I practice in my day job?
- How can I craft my day job to embed the new leadership skills I'd like to practice more?

You can assess your skills by reading the relevant literature, taking training, or having insightful discussions with your supportive network. Once you have assessed your mastery of each skill, you can devise a strategy to improve it. Theoretical learning with no hands-on practice does not contribute to acquiring knowledge.

DEVELOP YOUR NETWORK

The networking strategies you developed by volunteering are applicable at work. Don't leave them at the door of your office. You bump into a former colleague in the hallway? Practice small talk and active listening to learn more about what they are doing. Did you join an online meeting earlier? Chat with other participants to get to know them better and introduce yourself. Networking is both lateral (with your peers) and upward (with your management). It is a source of learning and support.

If you just landed in the project management world, you should begin to connect with more seasoned project leaders in your industry, both inside and outside your organization. If you are already a seasoned project leader, connect with new project leaders to mentor them and be reverse-mentored by them. Engage in fruitful discussions with thought leaders and treat each networking opportunity as a chance to learn.

EXPLORE NEW FIELDS

Volunteering has shown you that experimenting with new things helps you acquire leadership skills and develop a diverse network. To explore new fields at work, you need to:

- Reframe it as an experiment with a specific timeline.
- Look for mentors, buddies, and a supportive network.
- Define small steps you can take and compile a list of activities.

If you are in the early stages of your career as a project leader, you should explore new skills and experiment with different tools and behaviors. However, if you are a seasoned project leader, look for opportunities outside your area of expertise, while also seeking continuous improvement in your own area of expertise.

STAY EMPLOYABLE

Because of the dynamic nature of the work environment and the speed at which technology is changing, no one can expect to have the same job forever. While you are learning new leadership skills, expanding your network, experimenting, and taking charge of your project leadership path to remain employable, remember to keep adding value in your day job, and keep your door open to new employment opportunities. It is also important to embrace intentional curiosity. And you need to make sure your new skills and knowledge are visible, both within and outside your organization.

CASE STUDY: HOW CAN I BRING BACK MY VOLUNTEER EXPERIENCE INTO MY PROJECT CAREER?

Juan* is a technology project manager in the healthcare industry. Throughout his career, he's been honing his skills in various tech-related projects. Two years ago, he was assigned to oversee the technology security aspect of a company event.

Juan took the opportunity to network with his peers on the events team, demonstrating his interest in supporting the event's technological needs and learning more about them. During the event, he expressed his willingness to support upcoming events, recognizing them as invaluable learning opportunities.

Juan's passion for event organization grew exponentially with each event he worked on.

Realizing his new aspiration, he actively looked for a volunteer role in a projectized organization that hosts many events, hoping to lead the events team. Starting small, he collaborated with local project organizations to organize gatherings such as lunch and learn sessions and virtual webinars. In less than six months, he was the project manager for organizing a conference with more than 500 attendees.

Through these experiences, Juan discovered his affinity for creating event timelines and managing vendor relationships. He made a network of contacts within the events industry, and now, he is adding value to his own organization's events teams by sharing connections and lessons learned.

After a few years of volunteering as an event project manager, Juan is contemplating a potential shift from the tech department to the events team within his organization. Is he ready to make the move?

Our Views

Juan should start a conversation with events team members to inquire about upcoming open positions or potential opportunities for him to contribute, which will help him build a stronger relationship with them. Before formally requesting to transition to the events team, Juan should consider seeking mentorship from seasoned event managers within his organization.

The next step is for Juan to talk with his manager to discuss his career aspirations and interest in transitioning to the events team. He should highlight his expertise in event planning and vendor management and be honest about finding his passion as an event project manager.

By proactively engaging with the events team and his manager, Juan can navigate the transition and position himself for success in his new role as an event project manager in his own organization.

VOLUNTEERS' STORIES: RAMI KAIBNI IN CANADA

"I believe in giving back to the community, in project management as a profession, and in kindness and humanity." This is what Rami Kaibni told us. Rami is a senior project and development manager in a mid-sized project management consultancy company, and he has his own professional development and management consulting company, RMK Coaching.

Rami started volunteering through mentoring junior project managers, and that's when he noticed the positive impact this had on those beginning their journey in project management. It sparked his deep passion to expand his volunteering activities to help others.

Rami recognized the confusion and the need for guidance that individuals experience when beginning their careers. He strongly believes in the significant impact of giving back and how it could improve someone's professional path. Having learned things the hard way, Rami was motivated to assist others professionally and personally.

Since 2015, Rami has officially been involved in volunteering with various organizations, each offering unique opportunities for him to contribute and grow, including PMI, PMOGA, and PM4NGOs.

Rami's volunteering roles and activities are extensive and diverse. He is a mentor at PMI's Vancouver West Coast chapter, contributes to PMI Certification Development, and is one of PMI's LinkedIn Community Group moderators. Additionally, he serves as the PMOGA Canada Community Ambassador and one of the PMO Global Awards judges. Rami is also the senior network official for the International Association of Project Managers (IAPM) and responsible for Vancouver, Canada, and Jordan, and last, he is the Canada Hub Ambassador for PM4NGOs.

Looking back, Rami has one regret: "I wish I knew how rewarding volunteering was on both personal and professional levels, then I could have started volunteering earlier."

Rami recognizes that maintaining a good work–life balance, while also volunteering, can be challenging. However, he has honed his time management and multitasking skills to ensure he has time to engage with the different communities. Nevertheless, he acknowledges the need to recalibrate his priorities in the future if circumstances change in his personal or professional life.

Rami emphasizes that volunteering has been instrumental in his career development. Through his involvement, he has connected with experienced professionals who have guided him in project management, construction management, and leadership.

On a personal level, volunteering has provided Rami with the opportunity to grow on many levels. Interacting with individuals from different countries and backgrounds has helped him acquire cultural knowledge, improve his soft skills, and develop his emotional intelligence capability. He has also enhanced his self-awareness.

> For example, I thought I was an active listener, but at some point, I did discover that I am not, because active listening is more than just listening. It is one soft skill I worked hard to improve, which had tremendous positive impacts on my personal life.

Here is how Rami summarizes the essence of volunteering: "Volunteering within your field is a noble way to give back and reaffirm your commitment to the profession and community." He believes that individuals can uncover their true potential and experience personal and professional growth by volunteering.

As for knowing when to stop volunteering, Rami pays attention to his mental and physical health. When he detects the signals of an overwhelming workload, he reassesses his priorities and may wind down certain activities. Unless his well-being prohibits it, Rami rarely declines volunteer opportunities.

Rami ended our conversation with this advice:

> Volunteering is never a waste of time. It is an opportunity to learn, an opportunity to give back, and an opportunity to make a difference to yourself and others. Volunteering is as important as professional development because it contributes to personal and professional growth. Don't wait for the opportunities to present themselves; find them yourself.

KEY TAKEAWAYS

- Volunteering experiences can help you become a better project leader, but you need to have the right mindset and take time to pause and reflect.
- You can learn and hone leadership skills because you can practice them in a low-risk environment, and then, at work, you will have more confidence to apply them.

- You can improve your networking skills.
- You can explore new fields and develop a new mindset for work: experimenting is a way of learning.
- All these experiences will help you remain employable in a competitive world.

YOUR A.H.A. MOMENT: ACTIVITY, HOPE, ACTION

It's your turn!

ACTIVITY

Redo the self-assessment at the beginning of this book. Then ask yourself:

- What has changed?
- Why?
- What is your one key takeaway now?

HOPE

How do you hope to develop your career by volunteering?
Prompt: "By volunteering, I hope to …"

ACTION

During the next three months, keep a journal on how volunteering helps you acquire, hone, and develop leadership skills, build a more robust network, and explore new fields.

NOTE

1 Bennis, W. (2009). *On Becoming a Leader.* Hachette.

Afterword

Successful careers are not planned. They develop when people are prepared for opportunities because they know their strengths, their method of work, and their values. Knowing where one belongs can transform an ordinary person – hardworking and competent but otherwise mediocre – into an outstanding performer.[1]

Peter Drucker

When we began volunteering a few years ago, we did not realize that we were embarking on such a transformative journey. Like many people, we initially saw volunteering as a hobby, rather than something that could be used to advance our careers. But we were wrong. Neither of us had volunteered before, and we came from cultures (France in Yasmina's case and Spain in Mayte's) where volunteering is less valued in academia and the workplace. But we became project leaders, and one day, we wanted to expand our networks, practice different leadership skills, lead teams, and boost our creativity, and we realized that volunteering in projectized organizations would allow us to do this. Our paths crossed in the process, and we presented a webinar together about our volunteering experiences. It was an eye-opening experience. We were astonished by the waves we created. We decided to collaborate across the miles (Yasmina near Paris, and Mayte in Salt Lake City) before meeting face-to-face two years later. That's the power of volunteering to create unexpected long-term learning collaborations. We've gained so much transferable knowledge.

No one can predict the technological changes to come, but one thing is sure: as a project leader, you are on a nonstop journey of learning and career growth. Volunteering will equip you with the interpersonal skills to inspire and motivate people in various situations where you have to learn, adapt, and grow.

Through this book, we hope to have given you some keys to making the most of volunteering, by honing your leadership skills, meeting people beyond your usual circles, and exploring new territories.

This is the end of this book, but hopefully it is the beginning of an extraordinary volunteering journey for you – as it was for us. Volunteering is a rewarding way to connect deeply with others to impact the world positively.

Last but not least, if you want to share your own volunteering story, use **#volunteer2leader**.

If you have any questions or feedback, contact us on LinkedIn.

NOTE

1 Drucker, P. (2005, January). Managing Oneself. *Harvard Business Review Magazine.* https://hbr.org/2005/01/managing-oneself

Glossary

ACMP:	Association of Change Management Professionals
AIPM:	Australian Institute of Project Management
APEC:	Association pour l'Emploi des Cadres (French Association for the Employment of Executives)
BSC:	balanced scorecard
ERG:	Employee Resource Group
FOMO:	fear of missing out
IPMA:	International Project Management Association
PESTEL:	Political, Economic, Social, Technological, Environmental, and Legal
PMI:	Project Management Institute
PMO:	Project Management Office
PMOGA:	PMO Global Alliance
SMART:	Specific, Measurable, Achievable, Relevant, Time-bound
SWOT:	Strengths, Weaknesses, Opportunities, and Threats
VPMMA:	Veteran Project Manager Mentor Alliance

Index

Note: **Bold** page numbers refer to tables; *italic* page numbers refer to figures and page numbers followed by "n" denote endnotes.

Printed in the United States
by Baker & Taylor Publisher Services